CAMBRIDGE SCHOOL

Shakespeare

Stepping into Shakespeare

Practical ways of teaching Shakespeare to younger learners

Rex Gibson

CAMBRIDGE
UNIVERSITY PRESS

PUBLISHED BY THE PRESS SYNDICATE OF THE UNIVERSITY OF CAMBRIDGE
The Pitt Building, Trumpington Street, Cambridge, United Kingdom

CAMBRIDGE UNIVERSITY PRESS
The Edinburgh Building, Cambridge CB2 2RU, UK
40 West 20th Street, New York, NY 10011-4211, USA
10 Stamford Road, Oakleigh, VIC 3166, Australia
Ruiz de Alarcón 13, 28014 Madrid, Spain
Dock House, The Waterfront, Cape Town 8001, South Africa

http: www.cambridge.org

First published 2000
Reprinted 2001

Printed in the United Kingdom at the University Press, Cambridge

Typeface Baskerville and FF Meta *System* QuarkXPress®

A catalogue record for this book is available from the British Library

ISBN 0 521 775574

Prepared for publication by Gill Stacey
Designed by Richard Morris, Stonesfield Design

Illustrations by Adam Stower

Contents

The National Literacy Strategy

Shakespeare is a major resource for empowering all pupils' progress in literacy. *Stepping into Shakespeare* enables you to achieve all the objectives of the National Literacy Strategy as set out in the three strands of the NLS Framework: word, sentence and text.

WORD LEVEL

Shakespeare powerfully extends pupils' vocabulary. Every scene, however short, contains excellent opportunities for increasing their word knowledge. Shakespeare's unique language feeds pupils' delight in the relationships of sound and meaning. Pupils' spelling is assisted when they enact a scene, because their enjoyment combines with close attention to how individual words might be spoken in performance. Shakespeare motivates pupils' creativity as they experience how he revels in inventing new words, for example by using prefixes, suffixes and hyphens. The plays help pupils understand how words have changed over time, how Shakespeare brought thousands of new words into use in English, and how words which are now archaic (thou, thee, o'er, ere, etc.) are entirely appropriate in their dramatic context.

SENTENCE LEVEL

Shakespeare is unrivalled in his word play and use of powerful imagery to deepen the emotional effect on an audience. He loves surprising with unusual word order. His creativity serves as a model for increasing pupils' own linguistic power. They enjoy and learn from his use of puns, metaphors, similes, personifications, nouns as verbs, and other language devices. Shakespeare is the master of the active voice. The dramatic appeal of his language helps pupils understand complex sentence structure as they actively express nouns, adjectives and verbs, speaking and enacting his vivid statements, imperatives and questions. Shakespeare's sentence construction often differs from modern conventions of syntax, but because his sentences are made up of small units of meaning which can be performed in some way, he gives pupils active insight into grammatical structure.

TEXT LEVEL

Shakespeare powerfully aids pupils' comprehension and composition. In shared discussion, active presentations, and their own retellings, pupils understand how thought and action are embodied and expressed in language. As they enact scenes, speak the language in different ways, and engage in a variety of writing and design activities, pupils' personal responses are developed and sharpened, giving them insight into Shakespeare's distinctive language style. Shakespeare's playscripts give pupils access to the full range of dramatic and literary devices listed in the National Literacy Strategy: narrative, theme, monologue (soliloquy), dialogue, persuasive writing, verse, point of view, voice, rhyme, rhythm, stage directions, parody, and many other features. Every Shakespeare play shows how language creates character, and how meaning arises from context. Through activity and discussion, pupils grasp how each part is related to the whole: word to sentence, sentence to speech, speech to scene – and everything to that whole that is the play itself.

Introduction

This book is addressed to teachers of pupils aged between 9–13 years. It answers the two key questions those teachers ask:

Why teach Shakespeare to younger pupils?

How do I teach Shakespeare to younger pupils?

You may have never taught Shakespeare, or you may be a teacher with considerable experience of introducing Shakespeare to younger pupils. This book gives encouragement and support to those teachers who are about to teach Shakespeare for the first time. It also provides help to teachers who have already taught Shakespeare, deepening their knowledge and skills and opening up fresh possibilities for classroom work. Whatever your experience, you will be able to adapt and extend the many practical activities provided in *Stepping into Shakespeare* to ensure that they are suitable to the needs, aptitudes and abilities of your pupils.

Shakespeare may appear daunting if you have never taught it before, or if you have unhappy memories of how you encountered it when you were at school. But don't feel overwhelmed. You will find you can provide your pupils with an effective and enjoyable Shakespeare course using the resources provided here.

The major aims of *Stepping into Shakespeare* are to help your pupils enjoy their first encounters with Shakespeare, to improve their understanding, and to develop their literacy: their personal skills as readers, writers and speakers. To achieve those aims, the following pages contain all you need to teach Shakespeare's plays in actively structured, yet flexible ways that engage your pupils in imaginative enactments of Shakespeare's language, stories and characters.

Stepping into Shakespeare covers all aspects of teaching Shakespeare's plays to younger pupils, and gives particularly detailed help with Shakespeare's language. This is because teachers see language as the central characteristic of 'Shakespeare', but at the same time see it as the feature with which pupils need most help. The Teaching suggestions that accompany every script are therefore full of practical advice which enables teachers and pupils to turn Shakespeare's language from a disheartening enemy into a familiar and welcoming friend.

Do I have to be an actor or a 'Shakespeare expert'?

No special acting training is needed. Using the skills you already possess as a teacher will enable you to teach the lessons in *Stepping into Shakespeare*. Every teacher is already a 'performer' by virtue of the demands of the role. You will find yourself speaking as Macbeth or Miranda or Titania, but that doesn't mean putting on a false act, or pretending to be what you are not.

You don't have to be a 'Shakespeare expert'. You are an expert in teaching, and as you work with your pupils on the lessons in this book, your acquaintance with Shakespeare will become deeper and richer. All you need are the familiar professional qualities and skills of every good teacher of younger pupils: a love of language; the desire to help your pupils achieve their full potential in reading, speaking and writing; the ability to achieve that ambition in the classroom, presenting yourself and what you teach with integrity, truthfulness and enjoyment.

You can do it!

Why teach Shakespeare to younger pupils?

Shakespeare holds very special appeal for younger pupils. They respond to the plays with enthusiasm, readily suspending their disbelief as they imaginatively inhabit Shakespeare's inviting worlds. It's not difficult to identify the reasons that justify teaching Shakespeare to this age group.

Younger pupils gain huge enjoyment from Shakespeare. They revel in speaking the language, acting out scenes, and actively imagining themselves as characters. Their achievements bring them great feelings of satisfaction. Quite simply, it's fun!

Then there is the unique appeal of Shakespeare's stories, which possess an innate attraction for younger pupils. The plays are full of exciting events, strange twists and unfolding action. Just think of the opening scenes of the three plays in this collection: a dramatic shipwreck; three witches looking forward to their meeting with a great warrior; an angry father bursting into preparations for a wedding, demanding his daughter's death.

Similarly, Shakespeare's characters have a natural imaginative and dramatic appeal for younger pupils. In these three plays, they encounter a magician who was once a mighty duke, overthrown by his brother; an ambitious wife who urges her husband to kill his king and seize the crown; an Athenian workman who is magically transformed by a mischievous spirit into an ass, and who is loved by a queen.

Younger pupils respond readily to the themes of Shakespeare's plays. In the lessons in this collection, pupils can safely experience emotions of ambition and jealousy, anger and fear, love and hate. They can explore issues of fairness and justice (to whom does the island belong: Caliban or Prospero?), appearance and reality (false friendships, magical enchantments), loss and recovery, revenge and forgiveness.

Shakespeare also powerfully fosters pupil development: intellectually, imaginatively and emotionally. The plays extend pupils' vocabularies and add to their knowledge of literature, drama and the classics. In their enactments, in discussion, and in writing or design activities, pupils develop key skills in reading, writing, speaking and listening.

Shakespeare's language has huge appeal for younger pupils in its rhythms, sounds, vivid imagery and striking repetitions. Like the pupils themselves, the language is active and physical: 'Avaunt, and quit my sight', 'This island's mine!', 'Be not afeared, the isle is full of noises'.

So, can your pupils cope with Shakespeare?

Yes! Never underestimate how intelligently and imaginatively your pupils can respond to Shakespeare. High teacher expectation is one of the keys to successful school Shakespeare, and younger pupils have the ability and potential to rise to the challenge. The difficulties of Shakespeare are *enabling* difficulties. Mastering those difficulties gives pupils a palpable sense of achievement and self-esteem. You will find that the results can be thrilling and electrifying, as pupils make the language their own and bring the characters and stories to life in your classroom.

Teaching Shakespeare

The common objective of every lesson in this book is to help teachers enable their pupils to inhabit the imaginative worlds of Shakespeare's plays and so improve their literacy. The method used to achieve that objective is dramatic storytelling which releases the pupils' intelligence, emotions and imagination in a variety of active responses to Shakespeare's language, characters and stories. The method is firmly rooted in the nature of:

- Shakespeare: whose stories are told in active, physical language that invites being spoken and acted.

- Younger pupils: who delight in active, imaginative exploration of story, character and language.

- Classrooms: where large groups of pupils meet to learn under the guidance of a teacher.

In dramatic storytelling, teachers give pupils direct access to Shakespeare's language. Using a script in which Shakespeare presents a story or episode within a play, the teacher and the pupils speak the language, and enact it in a variety of ways.

This book contains all you need to introduce Shakespeare's plays to younger pupils. At least twelve lessons are provided for each of three plays: *A Midsummer Night's Dream*, *Macbeth*, *The Tempest*. Additional lessons 'For your delight' present a sonnet and extracts from other plays. Each can be used to increase pupils' enjoyment, appreciation and understanding.

Each lesson is presented as a double page spread. The left hand page is Shakespeare's script for photocopying so that every pupil in the class has their own personal copy. Every script is a 'story' of some kind, and the language is dramatic language, intensely physical and active. The words are an obvious invitation to acting out, to be spoken with accompanying expressions, gestures and movement. Pupils readily use the language to create character, atmosphere, meaning and feeling.

The right hand page is for the teacher. It contains the professional knowledge needed to help you teach the lesson. You can adapt or extend the Teaching suggestions to suit the particular needs and interests of your own pupils. Each lesson is structured into whole class, group,

and independent activities. Use your professional judgement to decide the amount of time you spend on each in any particular lesson. Many teachers have found it valuable to spread the work on a script over several lessons, so that groups have adequate time to prepare and show their presentations, and individual pupils can write at length.

Whole class: the teacher takes the lead, with all pupils participating in a variety of ways. The teacher's leadership helps pupils with speaking, understanding and enacting Shakespeare's language.

Group work: following whole class activity, pupils work in groups of suitable size. They take responsibility for rehearsal and delivery of their own version of the story in the script. They speak and express the language in imaginative enactments that are their own creations.

Independent work: individual pupils work on a wide variety of tasks which arise organically out of whole class and group work. This independent activity further enhances pupils' understanding and enactment of Shakespeare's language, characters and stories.

Twelve photocopiable worksheets are included for pupils' independent work. Each worksheet can be used with every script – so you have over 400 potential lessons available!

WHOLE CLASS

Ensure that every pupil has their own copy of the script. Each script is an episode in the play: a 'scene' which has dramatic and literary integrity in its own right. The script tells a coherent 'story', and is full of opportunities for a wide variety of language activities. Each script invites pupils to create an active presentation which develops from a clear beginning to a distinctive and dramatic end.

When working on Shakespeare with younger pupils, it is appropriate for the teacher to provide strong leadership and guidance in whole class sessions. You will find that the teacher's notes opposite each script suggest how your own presentation to the whole class might be done. The notes provide an introduction to the story and characters, and give explanations of unfamiliar words.

The teacher briefly sets the scene and selects pupil volunteers who will help with the demonstration of language and action. The teacher then speaks the language of the script in short sections, accompanying each section with actions, expressions and gestures that illuminate meaning. All pupils repeat the language and the actions. Most of the class are seated, but the 'volunteers', with the teacher directing, have greater freedom of movement.

As the teacher works through the script, the whole class plays an active role. All pupils speak the language, perform actions, and contribute ideas and suggestions about the characters, the unfolding story, and the delivery of the lines.

The teacher shows, by example, how any Shakespeare speech is made up of small units which can be clearly spoken and meaningfully acted. From the teacher's demonstration, pupils quickly learn how to identify these small units. When they work in groups or independently, pupils can divide the language into their own preferred units of meaning for speaking and acting out.

Dramatic storytelling is particularly effective in explaining unfamiliar words or phrases, because such explanations are best made in context, in action. Here, Shakespeare's language is exceptionally helpful. The small units of meaning can be spoken and enacted by the teacher in ways which aid pupils' understanding as they repeat the teacher's language and actions. Take, for example, these words from *The Tempest*:

> he needs will be
> Absolute Milan.

This can seem difficult on the page, but the meaning comes through clearly when the teacher stresses 'Absolute Milan', with special emphasis on 'absolute', and strikes a haughty pose as a great monarch, imperious and arrogant. Any accompanying verbal explanation can be brief: that Antonio ('he') thought of himself as absolutely in control of Milan, ruling entirely on his own, as a tyrant, and lording it over everyone in the city. Pupils will be ready, at the teacher's invitation, to strike a pose

as 'Absolute Milan'.

The teacher always identifies a small 'sense unit' that pupils can understand as they speak and physically act it in some way. That 'sense unit' may be a line of verse, but it can often be longer or shorter than the line. The important thing is to ensure that the chosen unit makes sense on its own. Many pupils can deal with quite long sense units, but it is best to begin with short units.

Another *Tempest* example illustrates how the short units of Shakespeare's language make it especially classroom-friendly in providing inviting opportunities for pupils to discuss, contribute ideas, and physically portray what is spoken:

> This foul witch Sycorax, … for mischiefs manifold,
> And sorceries terrible to enter human hearing,
> From Algiers, thou knowest, was banished.

- 'This foul witch Sycorax' – what does she look like?
- 'for mischiefs manifold' – pupils suggest and show some of her many wrongdoings.
- 'And sorceries terrible to enter human hearing' – pupils suggest and show the terrible spells and witchcraft that so appalled people.
- 'From Algiers, thou knowest, was banished' – the teacher points imperiously at the door, commanding a pupil to go outside. Such physical action conveys the meaning of 'banished' with little need for verbal explanation.

Similarly, the first few lines of 'The seven ages of man' from *As You Like It*, shows how small 'sense units' can aid dramatic presentation.

> All the world's a stage,
> And all the men and women merely players.
> They have their exits and their entrances,
> And one man in his time plays many parts,
> His acts being seven ages. At first the infant,
> Mewling and puking in the nurse's arms.

All the world's a stage	*sweeping dramatic gesture*
And all the men	*the boys take a bow*
and women	*the girls take a bow or curtsey*
merely players	*boys and girls strike a theatrical pose*
They have their exits	*make as if to leave the room*
and their entrances	*expansive 'entering' gestures*
And one man in his time plays many parts	*quickly pose as tragedy (sad), comedy (laughing), history (raise imaginary sword)*
His acts being seven ages	*pupils count to seven on fingers*
At first the infant	*rock a baby in your arms*
Mewling	*miaow like a cat*
and puking	*mime being sick*
in the nurse's arms	*register what you feel about baby being sick over you!*

After their active experience in whole class work, pupils will be ready to work in groups or pairs, when themselves choose the length of each language unit for acting out.

GROUP WORK

Group work is ideal for involving all pupils in practical activities and discussion. In the safety of the small group, pupils can draw on their own experience and culture, and make spoken and practical contributions that they may be reluctant to offer in whole class sessions. Group work enables pupils to gain ownership of Shakespeare's language as they take responsibility for the script, bringing story and character to active life in play and performance.

The main task for each group is to work out how they will stage their performance of the script. To achieve this objective, the teacher provides all kinds of guidance in the whole class session, and uses the Teaching suggestions to give additional help. To enable all groups to show and share some of their work with the whole class, some teachers allocate different sections of the script to different groups, or ask groups to report their plans, and to act out only a section of the script.

It is helpful to tell the groups that they are like Shakespeare's own Acting Company, The King's Men. This group of actors worked together on exactly the same task as the pupils: how do we perform this scene? To encourage pupil discussion and practical experiment, the teacher can remind groups of the questions that Shakespeare and his fellow-actors may have talked about as they worked on a scene:

- Should someone be the director – a leader and co-ordinator who helps everyone?
- Who plays which characters? Who speaks which lines?
- Can some or all of the lines be shared out, with several pupils speaking them together?
- How can you divide the language into small units, each of which can be spoken and acted in some way?
- How can you speak the language – loud or soft, fast or slow, tone of voice, which words to emphasise, etc.?
- Can you use choral speaking, echoing, and repetitions in your performance?
- What actions, gestures, and expressions might you use?
- How should each pupil move, relate to each other, respond to what is said?
- Should someone be a narrator? A narrator can introduce the scene in their own language, provide comments throughout and a final comment at the end.
- How will you begin the scene to stage a dramatic entry?
- How can you end the scene in a very dramatic way?
- What mood do you wish to create? Think about how you want the audience to respond to your performance.
- How can the group perform in the space allocated by the teacher?
- What costumes and props can be used? (Keep them simple!)

The teacher decides the size of group, depending on the requirements of the script and other considerations (e.g. control, time available, size of classroom). Pupils might work in pairs, for example sharing a speech or soliloquy as a conversation. Large groups can also work effectively. The number of characters in a scene is not always the best guide to group size, as several pupils might speak one character's lines, or you might wish each group to have a director and/or narrator. Knowing your own class, you will make appropriate judgements on how groups should be composed: pupils' free choice, teacher decision, or a mixture of the two.

INDEPENDENT WORK

Activities for individual pupils grow naturally out of whole class and group work. In writing and design activities, pupils develop key literacy skills. A host of personal writing opportunities immediately suggest themselves: stories and poems; writing from the point of view of a particular character; diary entries, letters to family or friends; writing as Shakespeare himself. It is often appropriate to devote a whole lesson to independent work to give pupils sufficient time for extended writing.

Pupils can mark up their scripts, writing notes and identifying words or phrases for special emphasis. They can summarise a scene (e.g. a synopsis in a given number of words); write parodies and character obituaries, speculate and hypothesise (what happens next?). Using Shakespeare's language as a model, pupils can invent additional dialogue or soliloquy (monologue). A single image or a favourite line can be a potent starting point for their own imaginative writing.

If you work through all the lessons on a play with your class, each pupil can clip their scripts together, adding any other written or illustrative work they have done. They can design a cover or folder for their collection, and so create a folder, journal or record of their Shakespeare work. The creation of such a document further increases the pupil's sense of ownership of Shakespeare and his or her involvement with the language, characters and stories.

The teacher's notes for each lesson suggests independent work relevant to the script. In addition, the 12 photocopiable worksheets (pages 96–107) increase the range of independent work. Each worksheet can be used with every playscript – providing a resource of over 400 lessons. Worksheets can be used in any order, but you may wish to choose the one you feel is of particular relevance at the particular point you have reached in structuring your pupils' Shakespeare experience. The worksheets invite pupils to step into a variety of roles and to express different points of view, all vitally concerned with Shakespeare:

- Storyboard your scene
  Pupils identify the moments and language the camera will capture.

- What's your title?
  Pupils write a poem or story inspired by Shakespeare's language.

- Step into character!
  Pupils reflect on their experience as a Shakespeare character.

- Become an actor at the Globe!
  The pupil becomes a member of Shakespeare's Acting Company.

- Director's notes
  The pupil steps into role as the director of the scene.

- Become a designer
  Pupils design a character's costume.

- Invent a narrator
  Pupils write the script for a narrator of their scene.

- You are William Shakespeare!
  Pupils get inside Shakespeare's mind!

- Write your review
  Pupils give their response to a performance.

- Edit your newspaper
  Pupils design the front page to report their scene.

- Design a handbill
  Pupils design a handbill advertising their scene.

- How I judge my work
  A self-assessment sheet for pupils to evaluate their achievements and contributions.

Shakespeare's language

Shakespeare was a poet who wrote drama, so the very sound of his language has special appeal for younger pupils. Every Shakespeare line has its own distinctive quality, inviting active expression. Pupils take genuine pleasure in discovering how they can bring characters and stories to life through Shakespeare's powerful words and rhythms of speech.

Shakespeare was always seeking out language to create characters and to enrich the imaginative and dramatic force of his plays. Younger pupils enjoy and respond to the fertile, atmospheric nature of Shakespeare's words and phrases. In discussion and in physical action they explore and invent different meanings and ways of acting out. Their performances frequently display that they have understanding of the language, even if the pupils themselves sometimes lack words to describe that understanding. Like adults, children know more than they can say.

Although much of Shakespeare's language is in fact familiar, it appeals to younger pupils because of its 'otherness', its strangeness, its difference from the everyday. His vocabulary and his syntax have a heightened, dramatic quality that pupils relish. They enjoy learning and speaking 'new' words and different sentence forms, and they quickly adjust to 'thou' and 'thee', accepting that such archaisms are appropriate to Shakespeare's plays.

Detailed help with language is given in the teaching notes opposite each script. The following brief reminders identify certain major features of Shakespeare's language of importance to teachers of younger pupils.

Imagery: imagery is the use of emotionally charged words and phrases which conjure up vivid mental pictures in the imagination ('Look like the innocent flower, but be the serpent under it'). Imagery helps to create the mood or atmosphere of a scene. It occurs as metaphor ('This cherry nose'), simile ('His eyes were green as leeks') and personification ('O lovely Wall'). Shakespeare's imagery is a powerful spur to pupils' imagination as they write their own poems or stories influenced by a particular image or images.

Repetition: Shakespeare uses all kinds of repetitions: words, phrases, rhythms, rhymes, vowel and consonant sounds (in assonance and alliteration): 'Fair is foul, and foul is fair'. As you teach any script, look out for repetitions that your pupils can exploit in some way as they speak and act.

Lists: Shakespeare loved 'piling up' language, accumulating item on item to increase dramatic effect. The most famous example is probably the list of ingredients that Macbeth's witches drop into their cauldron: 'Eye of newt, and toe of frog'. Many lists can be acted out by pupils, item by item.

Verse: Shakespeare's verse is written in 'five-beat rhythm' or iambic pentameter. This simply means that each line has five stresses or 'beats':

/   /   /   /   /
My mistress with a monster is in love

Pupils can clap or tap out the rhythm as they speak, or sway their hands or bodies gently to the rhythm.

If you really want to teach iambic pentameter to your pupils, choose your example carefully. Pages 24 and 94 ('My mistress ...' and Sonnet 18) are excellent, because both are in perfect iambic pentameter throughout. Unless you begin with a well-chosen example, pupils can become confused because Shakespeare often deliberately avoids writing in perfectly regular rhythm. Remember that younger pupils can enjoy, understand and appreciate Shakespeare without ever hearing the expression 'iambic pentameter'!

Some pupils enjoy a longer explanation of iambic pentameter. An iamb (or 'foot') is two syllables, one unstressed and the other stressed (as in birthday: birth**day**; envy: en**vy**; torment: tor**ment**; believe: bel**ieve**). Pentameter comes from the Latin 'penta' meaning five, and 'meter' meaning measurement of the rhythm of verse. So a line of iambic pentameter has ten syllables, five unstressed and five stressed.

As pupils pick up the rhythm, it can help them understand why Shakespeare sometimes shortens words, e.g. ne'er for never, o'er for over, or uses a grave accent (pavèd, fixèd) in order to maintain the rhythm of the line.

SPEAKING STYLES

In whole class sessions the teacher can give pupils help with variations in speaking style. The aim is to speak as effectively as possible, using appropriate tone, emphasis and style to convey clearly to the audience the meaning and emotional content of every line or short section of language. With that aim in view, all kinds of delivery can be explored to find a style that is dramatically appropriate. Such explorations include:

- varying the tempo: speaking fast or slowly
- varying the volume (whispering is not only dramatically effective, it also helps to keep discipline!)
- varying the emotional tone, speaking angrily, sadly, and so on
- emphasising key words and phrases
- stressing only one word in each line
- giving each word similar emphasis (particularly effective for single syllable lines)
- pausing, to add to the meaning and emotional impact of what has just been, or is about to be, said. Group work should always include pupils deciding where to pause.

WAYS OF SPEAKING

Teachers face a special problem that actors do not. An actor is given a part, and is the only person who speaks and performs it. But a school class has 20 to 30-plus pupils, and the teacher wants to give every one of them the experience of speaking and enacting the language in some way. The teacher uses whole class sessions to achieve that objective, demonstrating different ways of speaking and enacting a Shakespeare speech. For example, all the pupils speak together as they model the teacher's delivery of each section of the language, each of which is a coherent unit of meaning. Pupils draw on that experience in group work, where they explore ways of sharing the language. In addition to one pupil speaking alone, the possibilities include:

- Pupils work in pairs or threes, sharing a speech or a soliloquy as a conversation.
- A pair or group speak in unison.
- A group echoes particular words or phrases as one pupil speaks.
- A group repeats each phrase or line.
- A group adds a question or statement at the end of each line or phrase.
- A group echoes verbs, or adjectives, or nouns, or pronouns.
- The group adds 'backing' effects, intensifying the atmosphere of a speech, e.g. sound effects (owls hooting, bats squeaking, etc.), humming or providing some other quiet rhythmical backing accompaniment.
- All pupils speak together, pausing frequently. In the pauses all or some pupils perform a mime, perhaps in slow motion, or form a tableau to illustrate the words.
- Groups speak a line of verse at a time, emphasising the five-beat rhythm (de-dum, de-dum, de-dum, de-dum, de-dum), or four-beat rhythm for the witches' language or songs.

WHAT KIND OF VOICE?

Don't put on an artificial voice, and don't try to imitate the accent of the English upper middle class. There isn't a special 'Shakespeare voice' – even though some people think there is. Just use your own natural voice, but adjust it to the character, and the meaning and mood of the speech. Every Shakespearean king can speak in any accent or dialect, but there is usually a tone of authority in his voice because he is a monarch. Similarly, when Macbeth commands Banquo's Ghost 'Avaunt, and quit my sight!' his accent is immaterial, but his style of expression is vital. He is giving an urgent order, but he probably feels both fear and guilt.

The context of a speech always provides strong clues to how to speak. When Ariel says 'You are three men of sin' to the men who have overthrown Prospero, he is making a statement, but he speaks very emphatically and in a tone of condemnation, because he is about to 'judge' the three men. In a very different context, in *A Midsummer Night's Dream*, when Francis Flute the bellows-mender, playing Thisbe, says to the dead Pyramus, played by Bottom, 'What dead my dove? Asleep my love?' his questions are intended to evoke laughter from the audience. Here you might well use an artificial voice, because Flute is likely to be doing just that.

VOLUNTEERS – AND RELUCTANT PUPILS

Teachers tread a difficult tightrope in making use of pupils' talents in whole class sessions. The important thing is for every pupil to have the opportunity to speak and act. In every class there are always a number of 'natural' actors: pupils who relish the opportunity to put on a show to their fellow pupils. They volunteer at once for an acting part, and delight in speaking the language. Teachers should of course encourage and use these pupils in demonstrations. It develops their talents, and other pupils enjoy and learn from their performances. But look for ways to share the roles so that 'favouritism' (always using the same pupils) can be avoided.

There are other pupils in the class, less confident and self-assured, who are very reluctant to volunteer or to perform in front of their peers. Nonetheless, among these more diffident pupils are many who would love the opportunity to speak and act out the language. Seek ways to encourage them into volunteering.

The group and independent activities that are an integral part of the teaching strategy for younger pupils are excellent ways in which less confident pupils can be encouraged and developed. So too are the 'echoing' roles and other strategies in whole class work. Through such experience 'reluctant' pupils are more likely to volunteer in later lessons to take a more active part in class demonstrations.

Teacher's notes, scripts, worksheets

On the following pages you will find all you need to help you teach Shakespeare to younger pupils. There are scripts and teacher's notes for *A Midsummer Night's Dream*, *Macbeth*, *The Tempest* and for four lessons 'For your delight'. The 12 worksheets can each be used with all playscripts. Choose whichever one you feel is appropriate for pupils' independent work in any particular lesson.

Each lesson is presented as a double page spread. The right hand page is for you, the teacher. The left hand page is the script which you can photocopy so that every pupil has their own copy.

Story: a brief summary of the script

Characters: you may wish to prepare name labels for pupils who help in your whole class activity

Language: help with unfamiliar words. You may wish to write some or all on the board.

Some key characteristics of the language

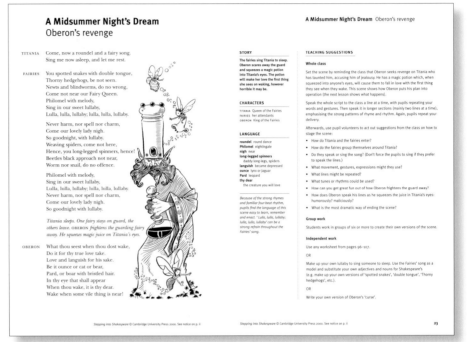

Teaching suggestions: giving you practical help with whole class, group and independent work. Use your professional judgement about how you manage time for these three activities. It is often helpful to spend two or three lessons on a script so that pupils have adequate time for group discussion, rehearsal and performance, and for extended writing in independent work time.

Worksheets

The photocopiable worksheets on pages 96–107 are for pupils' independent work. Every worksheet can be used with every playscript. Because the teacher's notes give a choice of independent work for nearly every script, you may decide not to use a worksheet if you prefer the alternative.

On each worksheet the pupil first writes name, date, play title and scene title (as given on the playscripts, e.g. 'Oberon's revenge').

A Midsummer Night's Dream

Macbeth

The Tempest

Four scripts 'For your delight'

As You Like It

Romeo and Juliet

The Two Gentlemen of Verona

The Sonnets

A Midsummer Night's Dream
Meet the characters

THESEUS (*Duke of Athens*)
Either prepare to die, or else to wed Demetrius.

HIPPOLYTA (*Queen of the Amazons*)
This is the silliest stuff that ever I heard.

EGEUS (*father of Hermia*)
Full of vexation come I.

HERMIA (*in love with Lysander*)
O me, you juggler, you canker-blossom, you thief of love.

HELENA (*in love with Demetrius*)
Fie, fie, you counterfeit, you puppet you!

LYSANDER (*who becomes muddled about who he loves*)
The course of true love never did run smooth.

DEMETRIUS (*who also gets muddled about who he loves*)
It seems to me that yet we sleep, we dream.

OBERON (*King of the Fairies*)
Ill met by moonlight, proud Titania!

TITANIA (*Queen of the Fairies*)
What, jealous, Oberon?

PUCK (*Oberon's attendant*)
I'll put a girdle round about the earth in forty minutes!

NICK BOTTOM THE WEAVER (*who plays Pyramus, a tragic lover*)
Let the audience look to their eyes: I will move storms.

PETER QUINCE THE CARPENTER (*who directs the play*)
Here's a marvellous convenient place for our rehearsal.

SNUG THE JOINER (*who plays Lion*)
Have you the lion's part written? Pray you, if it be,
give it to me, for I am slow of study.

 Stepping into Shakespeare © Cambridge University Press 2000. See notice on p. ii

STORY

This introductory lesson on characters enables pupils to explore and hypothesise what the story of the play might be.

CHARACTERS

As named on the pupils' script.

LANGUAGE

vexation irritation
juggler trickster
canker-blossom
    dog-rose or diseased flower
counterfeit false friend
put a girdle travel

This lesson uses active methods to introduce major characters in the play. It helps pupils discover how Shakespeare creates character through language, and it enables them to speculate about what the characters are like, how they interact and how the story might develop.

TEACHING SUGGESTIONS

Whole class

Tell the class that they are going to get acquainted with some of the characters in *A Midsummer Night's Dream* – and find out what they are like! Take each character in turn. Give pupils the name and brief description on the script, and speak their language. Pupils speak the line after you and strike a pose ('statue' or 'tableau') to portray the character who speaks. The portrayals can be done with pupils out of their seats, or sitting down if you prefer.

Don't be afraid to give all kinds of prompts. What sort of person says he can bring tears to an audience's eyes? Or what is someone like who asks a young woman to choose between marrying a man she dislikes or being executed?

Invite pupils to look at each others' 'statues' (this develops ideas about different ways of portrayal). Encourage class discussion of each character, asking pupils to give reasons for the sort of person they portray. Give the pupils plenty of practice, and use some of these guessing 'games':

- Choose a character (without telling the class). Strike a pose, without speaking – pupils guess which character is portrayed, and the language spoken.
- Speak a line – pupils name the character.
- Describe a character, e.g. 'Duke of Athens' – pupils name the character.
- Name a character – pupils speak the character's line, and strike a pose.
- Invite pupils to create their own story – what sort of play has these characters in it?
- Can pupils 'group' the characters? (Use your professional judgement about when you teach that there are three 'groups' in the play: court, spirit world, mechanicals.)

Group work

Pairs or small groups work through their scripts, trying out poses and speaking the language. They play the 'guess the character' activities above.

Independent work

Use the language to make up your own story of what happens in the play.

OR

Choose one character. Write what you think happens to him or her in the play.

OR

Draw a diagram showing how the characters 'group' together.

A Midsummer Night's Dream
The play in ten actions!

Either prepare to die, or else to wed Demetrius.

The course of true love never did run smooth.

Ill met by moonlight, proud Titania!

Wake when some vile thing is near!

What angel wakes me from my flowery bed?

How low am I, thou painted maypole?

My legs are longer though, to run away!

Now die, die, die, die, die!

And farewell friends,
Thus Thisbe ends,
Adieu, adieu, adieu!

Give me your hands, if we be friends,
And Robin shall restore amends.

A Midsummer Night's Dream The play in ten actions!

STORY

An opportunity for pupils to act out the whole play in ten actions!

CHARACTERS

As introduced in Teaching suggestions (right).

LANGUAGE

Ill met unpleasant meeting
painted maypole
   flashy tall person
restore amends
   in the future correct any errors

This is a lively and enjoyable introduction to the play. The vivid language from ten memorable moments in A Midsummer Night's Dream *gives pupils active opportunities to play major characters and to acquire a sense of the structure of the play from beginning to end.*

Using frequent dramatic pauses, the teacher narrates the story (as in Teaching suggestions, right), and speaks the lines, adding actions and expressions to help pupils' own speaking and actions. After each line, all the pupils, in pairs, step into role, repeat the line, and act it out.

TEACHING SUGGESTIONS

Whole class

Add to the following teacher commentary as you wish:

1   All is not well in Athens. Hermia refuses to marry Demetrius, the man her father has chosen for her. Duke Theseus passes a terrible judgement on Hermia: 'Either prepare to die, or else to wed Demetrius.' (Pupils speak and enact.)

2   Hermia decides to run away to a wood near Athens with her true love, Lysander. He tells the weeping Hermia: 'The course of true love never did run smooth.' (Pupils speak and enact.)

3   Meanwhile, in the wood, Oberon, King of the Fairies, angrily greets Titania, his Queen: 'Ill met by moonlight, proud Titania!' (Pupils speak and enact.)

4   Oberon is so angry with Titania that he squeezes a magic potion in her eye when she is asleep. It will make her love the first thing she sees on waking: 'Wake when some vile thing is near!' (Pupils speak and enact.)

5   And what is the first thing she sees? It's Bottom the weaver – and he is wearing an ass's head! But Titania loves him: 'What angel wakes me from my flowery bed?' (Pupils speak and enact.)

6   Meanwhile Hermia is quarrelling with her best friend Helena, who she thinks has stolen her true love, Lysander. And Helena has called her 'little'! 'How low am I, thou painted maypole?' (Pupils speak and enact.)

7   Helena is really scared of Hermia's anger. So, what does she do? 'My legs are longer though, to run away!' (Pupils speak and enact.)

8   But all the confusions are finally sorted out, and Bottom and his workmates perform their play before Duke Theseus. Bottom kills himself for love: 'Now die, die, die, die, die!' (Pupils speak and enact.)

9   Francis Flute the bellows-mender plays Bottom's true love, Thisbe. And she too kills herself for love! 'And farewell friends, Thus Thisbe ends, Adieu, adieu, adieu!' (Pupils speak and enact.)

10 Everything ends happily. Puck, the mischievous spirit who has caused so much confusion throughout the play, comes forward and asks the audience to applaud: 'Give me your hands, if we be friends, And Robin shall restore amends.' (Pupils speak and enact.)

Group work

In pairs or small groups, pupils rehearse and present 'the whole play'.

Independent work

Write the story of *A Midsummer Night's Dream*. Include all the language you have learned.

A Midsummer Night's Dream
An angry father

Enter DUKE THESEUS, QUEEN HIPPOLYTA *and*
the Athenian court.

THESEUS   Now, fair Hippolyta, our nuptial hour
Draws on apace. Four happy days bring in
Another moon. But O, methinks how slow
This old moon wanes!

HIPPOLYTA   Four days will quickly steep themselves in night.
Four nights will quickly dream away the time,
And then the moon, like to a silver bow
New bent in heaven, shall behold the night
Of our solemnities.

A regal procession around the stage, then EGEUS, HERMIA,
DEMETRIUS *and* LYSANDER *enter.*

EGEUS   Full of vexation come I, with complaint
Against my child, my daughter Hermia.
Stand forth Demetrius! My noble Lord,
This man hath my consent to marry her.
Stand forth Lysander! And my gracious Duke,
This man hath bewitched the bosom of my child.
Thou, thou, Lysander, at her window sung
With feigning voice verses of feigning love,
And stolen the impression of her fantasy
With bracelets of thy hair, rings, gauds, conceits,
Knacks, trifles, nosegays, sweetmeats.
With cunning hast thou filched my daughter's heart.
My gracious Duke,
I beg the ancient privilege of Athens,
As she is mine, I may dispose of her.
Which shall be either to this gentleman
Or to her death, according to our law.

HERMIA   I do entreat your grace to pardon me.

THESEUS   Take time to pause, and by the next new moon,
Upon that day either prepare to die,
Or else to wed Demetrius.

Theseus and all the court leave. Hermia and Lysander stay,
looking desolate.

A Midsummer Night's Dream An angry father

Stepping into Shakespeare © Cambridge University Press 2000. See notice on p. ii

STORY

Duke Theseus plans his wedding to Hippolyta. Egeus bursts in complaining about his daughter, Hermia. She refuses to marry the man he has chosen for her. Egeus demands she obey him or be executed. Theseus orders Hermia to marry as her father wishes or to pay the penalty.

CHARACTERS

THESEUS Duke of Athens
HIPPOLYTA Queen of the Amazons
EGEUS an Athenian nobleman
HERMIA his daughter
DEMETRIUS Egeus' choice for Hermia's husband
LYSANDER loved by Hermia
COURTIERS attending Duke Theseus

LANGUAGE

nuptial hour wedding day
apace speedily
wanes grows smaller
steep absorb, swallow
solemnities wedding ceremonies
vexation anger, irritation
feigning false, deceitful
impression of her fantasy signs of Hermia's love
gauds, conceits toys, trinkets
Knacks, trifles knicknacks, small gifts
nosegays, sweetmeats flowers, sweets
filched stolen

The language of Theseus and Hippolyta is formal and stately, suited to their dignity as Duke and Queen. In contrast, Egeus' language is angry and indignant, expressing his annoyance at his daughter's disobedience.

TEACHING SUGGESTIONS

Whole class

Work on each of the three episodes in turn. Choose pupil volunteers to act as the characters. Speak short sections of the script ('Now, fair Hippolyta', etc.), briefly explaining unfamiliar words. The whole class repeats your language and gestures, and contributes ideas on how the volunteers stage the action.

Duke Theseus and Queen Hippolyta look forward to their wedding. Remind the class that he has conquered her in battle, but fallen in love with her. How do they enter? Invite suggestions how to create a regal and dignified atmosphere to match their language. What pictures does Hippolyta's simile 'like to a silver bow new bent in heaven' (new crescent moon) conjure up in pupils' minds?

Egeus' entrance and complaint about his daughter's disobedience: pupils' responses to the following questions can guide your speaking and how the volunteers act the episode:

* How does each character enter?
* 'vexation' – how to speak the word to express Egeus' anger?
* 'Hermia' – how does Egeus speak her name to show what he thinks of her?
* 'Stand forth ...' – snap out each command?
* 'noble', 'gracious' – is he flattering Duke Theseus? What accompanying actions?
* 'Thou, thou Lysander' – how can you emphasise the scorn in each 'thou' ?
* 'bracelets of thy hair, rings, gauds, conceits, knacks, trifles, nosegays, sweetmeats' – what different tone of voice for each item to express Egeus' contempt for such cheap tricks?
* How does everyone react to Egeus' demand for his daughter's death?

Theseus' judgement: does he speak coldly and sharply, or as a regretful warning?

Group work

Pupils in groups of six or more try several 'read-throughs', taking turns to speak as the different characters (to give every pupil the chance to speak). Then rehearse a group performance to bring out the pomp and ceremony of the court, and the drama of Egeus' anger and Theseus' sentence of death.

Independent work

Use any worksheet from pages 96–107.

OR

Step into role as a courtier and write about what you saw and heard.

A Midsummer Night's Dream
Trouble ahead!

PUCK How now spirit, whither wander you?

FAIRY Over hill, over dale,
Thorough bush, thorough briar,
Over park, over pale,
Thorough flood, thorough fire;
I do wander everywhere,
Swifter than the moon's sphere,
And I serve the Fairy Queen,
To dew her orbs upon the green.
I must go seek some dewdrops here
And hang a pearl in every cowslip's ear.
Farewell, thou lob of spirits, I'll be gone,
Our Queen and all her elves come here anon.

PUCK The King doth keep his revels here tonight.
Take heed the Queen come not within his sight.
For Oberon is passing fell and wrath,
Because that she as her attendant hath
A lovely boy stolen from an Indian king,
She never had so sweet a changeling.
And jealous Oberon would have the child
Knight of his train, to trace the forests wild.
But she perforce withholds the lovely boy,
Crowns him with flowers, and makes him all her joy.
And now they never meet in grove or green,
By fountain clear or spangled starlight sheen,
But they do square, that all their elves for fear
Creep into acorn cups and hide them there.

STORY

In the enchanted wood near Athens, Puck challenges a Fairy, who tells of her services to Titania. Puck warns that Oberon and Titania quarrel every time they meet because Oberon is angry at Titania's refusal to give up an Indian boy to become his attendant.

CHARACTERS

PUCK a spirit who serves Oberon, King of the Fairies
FAIRY a spirit who serves Titania, Queen of the Fairies

LANGUAGE

pale fence
dew her orbs upon the green make fairy rings on the grass
lob lout, high-flier
anon very soon
passing fell and wrath mightily fierce and angry
changeling child stolen by fairies
train court
trace wander through
perforce by force
sheen gleam, shine
square quarrel, fight

This scene introduces the spirit world. It gives pupils the opportunity to explore Shakespeare's two verse styles in the play: four-beat rhythm (tetrameter) and five-beat rhythm (iambic pentameter).

TEACHING SUGGESTIONS

Whole class

This is the first sight of the spirit world of the play, the magical creatures who live in the enchanted wood near Athens. It is often helpful to begin with pupils' suggestions of what this magical forest and the strange spirits who inhabit it are like. How do such unreal characters move, speak and behave?

As always, the clues to the answers to such questions lie in Shakespeare's language, so give pupils the opportunity to speak it. Speak the lines yourself in a number of different styles, breathlessly, in a whisper, impatiently and so on, with pupils repeating your delivery. The Fairy's first eight lines can work well in pairs. Thereafter, a single line is the most effective unit for pupils to remember and repeat.

The scene shows how the spirit world is torn by the conflict between Oberon and Titania. Pupils enjoy exploring how that antagonism is expressed in the exchange between Puck and the Fairy. They can act out the story Puck tells.

If you wish to concentrate on Shakespeare's use of verse, the scene is excellent for introducing pupils to the two different metres. The Fairy's first nine lines are in the four-beat rhythm with which all pupils are already familiar:

    Over hill, over dale

The Fairy's last three lines, and Puck's lines, are in the five-beat rhythm of iambic pentameter: de-dum de-dum de-dum de-dum de-dum (see page 7). Give the pupils practice in speaking the lines in order to acquire the rhythm:

        /   /   /   /   /
    The king doth keep his revels here tonight.

Group work

Students work in pairs, taking turns to speak as each character and working out their plans for staging the encounter between Puck and the Fairy.

Independent work

Use any worksheet from pages 96–107.

OR

Make up four or more lines of verse in five-beat rhythm (iambic pentameter). The lines can be about the quarrel of Oberon and Titania, or about yourself:

        /   /   /   /   /
    My birthday is the twenty first of May.

A Midsummer Night's Dream
Jealousy!

Enter OBERON *and* TITANIA *with their attendants.*

OBERON   Ill met by moonlight, proud Titania!

TITANIA   What, jealous Oberon? Fairies skip hence.

OBERON   Titania, I know thy love to Theseus.

TITANIA   These are the forgeries of jealousy,
And never since the middle summer's spring,
Met we on hill, in dale, forest, or mead,
By pavèd fountain or by rushy brook,
Or in the beachèd margent of the sea,
To dance our ringlets to the whistling wind,
But with thy brawls thou hast disturbed our sport.
Therefore the winds, piping to us in vain,
As in revenge have sucked up from the sea
Contagious fogs, which, falling in the land,
Hath every pelting river made so proud
That they have overborne their continents.
The ox hath therefore stretched his yoke in vain,
The ploughman lost his sweat, and the green corn
Hath rotted ere his youth attained a beard.
The fold stands empty in the drownèd field,
And crows are fatted with the murrion flock.
The nine-men's morris is filled up with mud,
And the quaint mazes in the wanton green
For lack of tread are indistinguishable.
The human mortals want their winter cheer,
No night is now with hymn or carol blessed.
And thorough this distemperature we see
The seasons alter. The spring, the summer,
The childing autumn, angry winter change
Their wonted liveries, and the mazèd world
By their increase now knows not which is which.
And this same progeny of evils comes
From our debate, from our dissension.
We are their parents and original.

A Midsummer Night's Dream Jealousy!

STORY

Oberon accuses Titania of being in love with Theseus. She claims he is jealous, and that his jealousy has caused all kinds of disasters in the natural world.

CHARACTERS

OBERON King of the Fairies
TITANIA Queen of the Fairies
ATTENDANTS to the King and
   Queen

LANGUAGE

forgeries lies
mead meadow
pavèd pebbled
beachèd margent shoreline
ringlets circular dances
Contagious disease-carrying
pelting unimportant
overborne their continents
   flooded over their banks
stretched his yoke
   pulled the plough
fold sheep-fold
murrion flock diseased sheep
nine-men's morris
   an outdoor game, like draughts
   or checkers, where the 'board'
   is holes cut into the grass
wanton green lush grass
want lack
distemperature disorder
childing fruitful
wonted liveries usual dress
mazèd amazed
progeny children
dissension quarrel

Titania's language conjures up vivid pictures of disorder in the countryside.

TEACHING SUGGESTIONS

Whole class

Titania tells of the effects of Oberon's jealousy. Wherever she and her attendants met, his violent behaviour upset their dances. The result of their quarrels is foul weather which has caused ruined harvests, diseased sheep, and desolation everywhere. Men and women are unhappy and all the seasons are confused. Every disturbance stems from the quarrels and jealousies of Oberon and Titania.

Titania's speech is a very poetic description of the devastating results of her quarrel with Oberon. It may not seem dramatic, but it offers fruitful opportunities for choral speaking and sound effects, and for group and independent work on the rich language. Here is just one way of working.

Divide the whole class into four groups, each of which will speak in turn. Speak a short section at a time, and point at one of the groups to repeat after you:

- 'Ill met by moonlight, proud Titania' – use a menacing tone.

- 'What, jealous Oberon?' – spoken mockingly.

- 'Fairies skip hence' – make it an imperious command.

Titania's speech can be divided up, sometimes into very short sections, e.g.: 'Met we on hill,' (point upwards), 'in dale,' (point downwards), 'forest, or mead,' (point) etc. Sometimes you might make a single word the spoken unit, e.g. 'Therefore' (spoken emphatically).

It is possible to enact sections of the speech, and to accompany others with sound effects. To help the class see how it might be done, direct a few pupil volunteers: showing how Oberon interrupts the dance; quietly but menacingly humming through 'Therefore the winds ... continents'; pulling the plough, etc.

Group work

Small groups work out a choral speaking delivery of the scene. Alternatively, you may prefer to give each group a short section of the script to speak and enact in some way. It can divide into: 'These are ... sport.' (7 lines); 'Therefore ... continents.' (5 lines); 'The ox ... indistinguishable.' (8 lines); 'The human mortals ... which.' (7 lines); 'And this same ... original.' (3 lines).

Independent work

Use any worksheet from pages 96–107.

OR

Write a poem about how jealous quarrels turns today's world upside down. Use Titania's speech as a model for your poem.

A Midsummer Night's Dream
Oberon's revenge

TITANIA   Come, now a roundel and a fairy song.
   Sing me now asleep, and let me rest.

FAIRIES   You spotted snakes with double tongue,
   Thorny hedgehogs, be not seen.
   Newts and blindworms, do no wrong,
   Come not near our Fairy Queen.
   Philomel with melody,
   Sing in our sweet lullaby,
   Lulla, lulla, lullaby; lulla, lulla, lullaby.

   Never harm, nor spell nor charm,
   Come our lovely lady nigh.
   So goodnight, with lullaby.
   Weaving spiders, come not here,
   Hence, you long-legged spinners, hence!
   Beetles black approach not near,
   Worm nor snail, do no offence.

   Philomel with melody,
   Sing in our sweet lullaby,
   Lulla, lulla, lullaby; lulla, lulla, lullaby.
   Never harm, nor spell nor charm,
   Come our lovely lady nigh.
   So goodnight with lullaby.

*Titania sleeps. One fairy stays on guard, the
others leave.* OBERON *frightens the guarding fairy
away. He squeezes magic juice on Titania's eyes.*

OBERON   What thou seest when thou dost wake,
   Do it for thy true love take.
   Love and languish for his sake.
   Be it ounce or cat or bear,
   Pard, or boar with bristled hair.
   In thy eye that shall appear
   When thou wake, it is thy dear.
   Wake when some vile thing is near!

STORY

The fairies sing Titania to sleep. Oberon scares away the guard and squeezes a magic potion into Titania's eyes. The potion will make her love the first thing she sees on waking, however horrible it may be.

CHARACTERS

TITANIA Queen of the Fairies
FAIRIES her attendants
OBERON King of the Fairies

LANGUAGE

roundel round dance
Philomel nightingale
nigh near
long-legged spinners
  daddy long-legs, spiders
languish became depressed
ounce lynx or jaguar
Pard leopard
thy dear
  the creature you will love

Because of the strong rhymes and familiar four-beat rhythm, pupils find the language of this scene easy to learn, remember and enact. 'Lulla, lulla, lullaby; lulla, lulla, lullaby' can be a strong refrain throughout the Fairies' song.

TEACHING SUGGESTIONS

Whole class

Set the scene by reminding the class that Oberon seeks revenge on Titania who has taunted him, accusing him of jealousy. He has a magic potion which, when squeezed into anyone's eyes, will cause them to fall in love with the first thing they see when they wake. This scene shows how Oberon puts his plan into operation (the next lesson shows what happens).

Speak the whole script to the class a line at a time, with pupils repeating your words and gestures. Then speak it in longer sections (mainly two lines at a time), emphasising the strong patterns of rhyme and rhythm. Again, pupils repeat your delivery.

Afterwards, use pupil volunteers to act out suggestions from the class on how to stage the scene:

- How do Titania and the Fairies enter?
- How do the Fairies group themselves around Titania?
- Do they speak or sing the song? (Don't force the pupils to sing if they prefer to speak the lines.)
- What movement, gestures, expressions might they use?
- What lines might be repeated?
- What tunes or rhythms could be used?
- How can you get great fun out of how Oberon frightens the guard away?
- How does Oberon speak his lines as he squeezes the juice in Titania's eyes: humorously? maliciously?
- What is the most dramatic way of ending the scene?

Group work

Students work in groups of six or more to create their own versions of the scene.

Independent work

Use any worksheet from pages 96–107.

OR

Make up your own lullaby to sing someone to sleep. Use the Fairies' song as a model and substitute your own adjectives and nouns for Shakespeare's (e.g. make up your own versions of 'spotted snakes', 'double tongue', 'Thorny hedgehogs', etc.).

OR

Write your own version of Oberon's 'curse'.

A Midsummer Night's Dream
Puck works his mischief!

My mistress with a monster is in love.
Near to her close and consecrated bower,
While she was in her dull and sleeping hour,
A crew of patches, rude mechanicals,
That work for bread upon Athenian stalls,
Were met together to rehearse a play,
Intended for great Theseus' nuptial day.
The shallowest thick-skin of that barren sort,
Who Pyramus presented, in their sport
Forsook his scene and entered in a brake,
When I did him at this advantage take.
An ass's nole I fixed upon his head.
Anon his Thisbe must be answerèd,
And forth my mimic comes. When him they spy –
As wild geese that the creeping fowler eye
Or russet-pated choughs, many in sort,
Rising and cawing at the gun's report,
Sever themselves and madly sweep the sky –
So at his sight away his fellows fly.
And at our stamp here o'er and o'er one falls,
He 'Murder!' cries, and help from Athens calls.
Their sense thus weak, lost with their fears thus strong,
Made senseless things begin to do them wrong,
For briars and thorns at their apparel snatch,
Some sleeves, some hats; from yielders all things catch.
I led them on in this distracted fear,
And left sweet Pyramus translated there.
When in that moment, so it came to pass,
Titania waked, and straightway loved an ass.

A Midsummer Night's Dream   Puck works his mischief!

STORY

Puck tells how the mechanicals met to rehearse a play near the sleeping Titania. Puck fixed an ass's head on Bottom. The sight of it scared away all his friends. But when Titania woke, the magic potion that Oberon had squeezed into her eyes made her fall instantly in love with the transformed Bottom!

CHARACTERS

PUCK a spirit
TITANIA Queen of the Fairies
BOTTOM the weaver
MECHANICALS Bottom's fellow workmen: Peter Quince the carpenter; Francis Flute the bellows-mender; Tom Snout the tinker; Robin Starveling the tailor; Snug the joiner

LANGUAGE

close and consecrated bower
  secret and holy shaded place
patches clowns
rude mechanicals
  rough workmen
barren sort foolish gang
Forsook left
a brake bushes
ass's nole head of a donkey
fowler bird hunter
russet-pated choughs
  grey-headed birds
many in sort in a great flock
Sever scatter
at our stamp
  as I stamped my foot
apparel clothes
yielders cowards
translated transformed

The strong rhymes and utterly regular rhythm make Puck's story easy to learn and act. And it's full of fun!

TEACHING SUGGESTIONS

Whole class

Use the Story (left) to set the scene in as much detail as you feel appropriate. Titania is asleep, her eyes bewitched by a love potion. Choose volunteers to act as characters. Speak each short section, with the whole class repeating your words. The volunteers act out suggestions from you and the pupils. Some hints:

- 'My mistress with a monster is in love.' The whole class, in pairs, can show their 'statues' of Titania and Bottom (they need not get out of their seats).
- 'Near ... hour' – Titania sleeps.
- 'A crew ... day' – lots of action to express the detail of each line. How do they enter, demonstrate their trades (see Characters, left), begin to rehearse?
- 'The shallowest ... sort,' – Bottom takes a bow.
- 'Who Pyramus presented,' – briefly explain Pyramus (a young lover in ancient Greece).
- 'in their sport ... head.' – Bottom leaves, and Puck fixes an ass's head on him. It adds to pupils' enjoyment if you produce the pair of ass's ears that you have made before the lesson. A card band with a pair of paper ears takes only a few minutes to construct.
- 'Anon ... answerèd,' – Thisbe (Francis Flute), calls 'Pyramus, Pyramus'.
- 'And forth my mimic comes.' – a grand entrance by Bottom!
- 'When him they spy ... catch.' Work through these 12 lines a short section at a time, helping pupils to express all the fearful action embodied in the language: wild geese flying from a hunter; flocks of birds scattering; one mechanical falling, one shouting; all being scratched by briars and losing some of their clothing. Slow motion performance adds to the fun!
- 'I led them on ... there.' – Puck leads mechanical away, leaving only Bottom, who looks confused and disbelieving.
- 'When in that moment .. ass.' – ask for suggestions how to make the awakening and falling in love as funny as possible.

Group work

Groups of six or more prepare their own version of the scene, beginning and ending with the glorious moment when Titania wakes, sees Bottom wearing the ass's head that Puck has fixed on him, and instantly falls in love!

Independent work

Use any worksheet from pages 96–107.

OR

Tell the story in exactly 50 words.

A Midsummer Night's Dream
Hermia versus Helena

HELENA   Injurious Hermia, most ungrateful maid,
Have you not set Lysander, as in scorn
To follow me, and praise my eyes and face?
And made your other love, Demetrius,
To call me goddess, nymph, divine and rare.

HERMIA   I understand not what you mean by this.

HELENA   Ay, do! Persever, counterfeit sad looks,
Make mouths upon me when I turn my back.
Wink at each other, hold the sweet jest up.

*Lysander and Demetrius show their adoration of Helena, and Lysander
rejects Hermia. She suddenly thinks that Helena has stolen his love.*

...Most ungrateful maid...
... she is something lower
than myself...

...you canker-blossom...
...you thief of love...

HERMIA   O me, you juggler, you canker-blossom,
You thief of love!

HELENA   Fie, fie, you counterfeit, you puppet, you!

HERMIA   'Puppet'? Why so? Ay, that way goes the game.
How low am I thou painted maypole? Speak!
How low am I? I am not yet so low
But that my nails can reach unto thine eyes.

HELENA   Let her hurt me not. Let her not strike me
Because she is something lower than myself.

HERMIA   Lower? Hark, again!

HELENA   O, when she is angry she is keen and shrewd.
She was a vixen when she went to school.
And though she be but little, she is fierce.

HERMIA   Little again? Nothing but low and little?
Let me come to her.

HELENA   I will not trust you, I,
Your hands than mine are quicker for a fray,
My legs are longer though to run away!   (*She runs off*)

HERMIA   I am amazed, and know not what to say.

STORY

Helena accuses Hermia of mocking her by making Lysander and Demetrius pretend to love her. But Hermia accuses Helena of stealing the love of Lysander, and becomes enraged when Helena calls her 'little'.

CHARACTERS

HERMIA in love with Lysander
HELENA in love with Demetrius
LYSANDER and DEMETRIUS who once loved Hermia, but whose eyes have been bewitched with a potion so that they are now both in love with Helena

LANGUAGE

nymph beautiful spirit
Persever persevere, continue (with your tricks)
counterfeit pretend
Make mouths pull faces
hold the sweet jest up keep the joke going
canker-blossom diseased flower
keen and shrewd sharp and bad-tempered
vixen female fox, bad-tempered
fray fight

The conflict and insults provide an exciting opportunity for the class to divide into pairs and quarrel in Shakespeare's language!

TEACHING SUGGESTIONS

Whole class

Set the scene by telling the story so far. Lysander and Demetrius were both in love with Hermia, but in the forest, Puck and Oberon have squeezed magic juice into their eyes, causing both of them to fall in love with Helena. Helena thinks a trick is being played on her – and one thing leads to another!

First, give the class the opportunity to insult their teacher! Speak the second half of the script (from 'O me, you juggler') in short sections, with the class repeating after you. Pupils get much enjoyment from having the chance to call their teacher 'thou painted maypole', etc.

Then choose four volunteers to act as the characters. Lysander and Demetrius do not speak, but have plenty to do. They show how much they love Helena, and they restrain Hermia from attacking Helena as she becomes angrier and angrier. Work through the whole scene using pupils' suggestions to direct the volunteer actors, e.g.:

- 'Injurious Hermia ... maid,' – Hermia looks puzzled.
- 'Have you ... face?' – Lysander acts out showing love.
- 'And made ... rare.' – Demetrius also shows love, and can repeat 'goddess', 'nymph', 'divine', 'rare'.
- 'Ay, do! ... jest up.' – bold actions and expressions to show 'sad looks', 'Make mouths', 'Wink', 'hold ... up'.

The stage direction and the following quarrel between Hermia and Helena can be enacted in all kinds of ways. The sheer energy of their language will ensure lively classroom rehearsal.

Group work

It is vital that every pupil gets the chance to speak Hermia's and Helena's powerful language. So first have the class working in pairs, speaking the script to each other, in a variety of ways: faces close together, whispering, back to back, etc. Pairs can then combine into groups of four to work out how to stage their versions of the episode.

Independent work

Use any worksheet from pages 96–107.

OR

Invent language for Lysander and Demetrius to speak in this scene.

A Midsummer Night's Dream
Presenting the play

Gentles, perhaps you wonder at this show,
But wonder on, till truth makes all things plain.
This man is Pyramus, if you would know.
This beauteous lady Thisbe is, certain.
This man with lime and rough-cast doth present
Wall, that vile wall which did these lovers sunder.
And through Wall's chink, poor souls, they are content
To whisper – at the which let no man wonder.
This man with lanthorn, dog, and bush of thorn,
Presenteth Moonshine. For, if you will know,
By moonshine did these lovers think no scorn
To meet at Ninus' tomb, there, to woo.
This grisly beast, which Lion hight by name,
The trusty Thisbe, coming first by night,
Did scare away, or rather did affright.
And as she fled, her mantle she did fall,
Which Lion vile with bloody mouth did stain.
Anon comes Pyramus, sweet youth and tall,
And finds his trusty Thisbe's mantle slain.
Whereat, with blade, with bloody, blameful blade,
He bravely broached his boiling bloody breast.
And Thisbe, tarrying in mulberry shade,
His dagger drew, and died. For all the rest,
Let Lion, Moonshine, Wall, and lovers twain,
At large discourse, while here they do remain.

Stepping into Shakespeare © Cambridge University Press 2000. See notice on p. ii

STORY

Peter Quince tells the plot of the play, presenting each actor in turn, and explaining what happens. Pyramus and Thisbe whisper through the wall and arrange to meet at Ninus' tomb. At the tomb, the lion scares Thisbe away, and Pyramus, believing she is dead, slays himself. Thisbe, finding him dead, also kills herself.

CHARACTERS

PETER QUINCE narrator
BOTTOM Pyramus
FLUTE Thisbe
SNUG Lion
STARVELING Moonshine
SNOUT Wall

LANGUAGE

Gentles Ladies and Gentlemen
lime and rough-cast
  building materials
sunder keep apart
lanthorn lantern
think no scorn believe it right
hight is called
mantle cloak
tarrying in mulberry shade
  waiting under a mulberry tree
twain two
At large discourse
  publicly present as a play

Peter Quince's prologue to the play of Pyramus and Thisbe offers pupils rich opportunities for comic invention. It contains a glorious parody of alliteration ('bloody, blameful blade …').

TEACHING SUGGESTIONS

Whole class

Set the scene: the mechanicals are about to present their play to Duke Theseus and his court. Peter Quince speaks this prologue, which introduces the characters and tells the story. Step into role as Peter Quince and speak the prologue in short sections. The whole class repeats your words and actions. Give any necessary explanations briefly. Use pupil volunteers to act out each section, inviting class suggestions about how characters behave. Some hints:

- 'Gentles' – does Quince bow? Is he confident or nervous speaking to the court?
- 'This man is Pyramus,' – Bottom, full of confidence, takes a bow!
- 'This beauteous lady Thisbe is,' – but Thisbe is Flute the bellows-mender who is extremely unhappy at having to play a woman! How does he present himself?

Carry on working through the prologue, asking for pupils' suggestions, e.g. How does Wall respond to being called 'vile wall'? How does he present a 'chink' through which the lovers whisper? Can a pupil play Moonshine's dog? 'Ninus' tomb' can be a tableau of two or three pupils who pose as a monument.

Exploit the rich language opportunities:

- 'grisly beast' – ensure you get plenty of alternative suggestions for the adjective: frightful, ghostly, gruesome, macabre, hideous, ghoulish – and more!
- 'which Lion hight by name' – the old-fashioned word 'hight' (called) can become a class joke. For example, Lion can take a bow and say 'I'm hight Lion, but I'm hight Snug the joiner really.'

Make sure all the pupils get the chance to speak and relish Shakespeare's 'send up' of alliteration in 'Whereat, with blade, with bloody, blameful blade, He bravely broached his boiling bloody breast.'

Group work

Groups of six or more pupils work out their own performance of the lines. Remind them to allow sufficiently long pauses between each short section in which the language can be acted out in as hilariously as possible.

Independent work

Use any worksheet from pages 96–107.

OR

Make up a sentence, full of alliteration, for Bottom to speak. Then make up different alliterative sentences for each of the characters.

A Midsummer Night's Dream
Die, die, die, die, die!

FLUTE (as THISBE) This is old Ninny's tomb. Where is my love?

SNUG *enters, as* LION. *He roars, Thisbe runs off, dropping her mantle. Lion savages the mantle, then exits.* BOTTOM *enters as* PYRAMUS.

BOTTOM Sweet moon, I thank thee for thy sunny beams.
I thank thee, moon, for shining now so bright.
For by thy gracious, golden, glittering gleams,
I trust to take of truest Thisbe sight.
But stay – O spite!
But mark, poor Knight,
What dreadful dole is here?
Eyes, do you see?
How can it be?
O dainty duck, O dear!
Thy mantle good –
What, stained with blood?
Approach, ye Furies fell!
O Fates, come, come,
Cut thread and thrum,
Quail, crush, conclude, and quell!
Come tears, confound!
Out sword and wound
The pap of Pyramus,
Ay, that left pap
Where heart doth hop.
Thus die I, thus, thus, thus!
(*Stabs himself*)
Now am I dead,
Now am I fled.
My soul is in the sky.
Tongue, lose thy light,
Moon, take thy flight.
Now die, die, die, die, die!
(*He dies*)

STORY

The mechanicals are acting the play of Pyramus and Thisbe. The lovers have arranged to meet at Ninus' tomb, but Thisbe is frightened away by the lion. Pyramus, played by Bottom, thinks Thisbe is dead. He kills himself for love.

CHARACTERS

FLUTE Thisbe
SNUG Lion
BOTTOM Pyramus

LANGUAGE

Ninny's tomb Ninus' tomb
mantle cloak
dreadful dole terrible grief
Furies avenging goddesses who punish crimes
fell deadly, cruel
Fates three goddesses who wove, then cut the 'thread and thrum' (woven cloth) of each human life
Quail languish, weaken
quell kill
pap nipple

Shakespeare may be mocking his teachers who insisted that he learned all about alliteration, rhyme and repetition! Bottom's speech parodies all those uses of language. Your pupils will enjoy the spoof!

TEACHING SUGGESTIONS

Whole class

Remind the class of the context. The mechanicals are acting out their play in front of Duke Theseus and his court. Their play is a burlesque of a classical story. Shakespeare is poking fun at serious plays (like *Romeo and Juliet*) that end in the death of the lovers. So he writes a speech that is intended to make the audience laugh, and Bottom 'goes over the top' as he tries to imitate the language and style of high tragedy.

Have two volunteers as Flute (Thisbe) and Snug (Lion) act out the opening line and stage direction. Encourage the class to offer advice on how to make the episode as funny as possible.

Then step into role as Bottom and give a performance full of bad acting: lots of exaggerated gestures and poses. The pupils repeat your words and actions. Your objective is, through enjoyment, to help the pupils understand the main language features of the speech: the repetitions of alliteration, rhyme and rhythm. You can achieve this practically, rather than through explanation and analysis. In the whole class session, the task is for the pupils to emphasise and enjoy the repetitions. Identifying the patterns can be done in group and independent work if you wish (there are other kinds of repetitions in the script: repeated words and phrases, questions, sentence forms).

- Make the most of the alliteration in the third line, emphasising each of the 'g's: 'gracious, golden, glittering gleams'. The speech is packed with alliterative lines that can provoke laughter as Bottom revels in them.

- The rhymes and rhythms are equally obvious. There's much humour to be gained for example, as Bottom tries to rhyme 'confound' and 'wound'.

- Make your explanation of 'Furies fell!' and 'Fates ... thread and thrum' brief. Greek classical mythology might be a follow-up for some students.

- It adds to the hilarity if, in the final line, Bottom accompanies each 'die' with a different action.

Group work

Groups of three or more work out their own performance. Encourage groups to give everyone the chance to speak and act Bottom's lines.

Independent work

Use any worksheet from pages 96–107.

OR

Write a poem about Bottom that begins ' O dainty duck, O dear!'

A Midsummer Night's Dream
Thisbe's grand farewell

Asleep, my love?
What, dead, my dove?
O Pyramus, arise.
Speak, speak! Quite dumb?
Dead, dead? A tomb
Must cover thy sweet eyes.
These lily lips,
This cherry nose,
These yellow cowslip cheeks,
Are gone, are gone,
Lovers make moan,
His eyes were green as leeks.
O sisters three,
Come, come to me,
With hands as pale as milk.
Lay them in gore,
Since you have shore
With shears his thread of silk.
Tongue not a word!
Come, trusty sword,
Come blade, my breast imbrue! (*Stabs herself*)
And farewell, friends,
Thus Thisbe ends,
Adieu, adieu, adieu! (*Dies*)

STORY

The mechanicals are almost at the end of their play. Pyramus (Bottom) has slain himself, thinking a lion has killed his beloved Thisbe. But Thisbe (Flute) is alive. She ran away from the lion, and now returns to find Pyramus dead. She grieves over him, then kills herself with his sword.

CHARACTERS

THISBE played by Flute
PYRAMUS played by Bottom

LANGUAGE

sisters three the three Fates, goddesses who wove the thread of human lives
gore blood
shore cut (the Fates ended human lives by cutting the threads of silk they had woven)
imbrue stain with blood

Thisbe's speech is made up of four stanzas, each with six lines. Pupils enjoy the short sentences and strong rhymes and rhythms. The ridiculous comparisons (e.g. 'cherry nose' = metaphor, 'eyes were green as leeks' = simile) add to the fun.

TEACHING SUGGESTIONS

Whole class

Remind the class of the context. The mechanicals are playing before Duke Theseus and they want to copy the serious language and atmosphere of tragic plays. Their play is rather like the end of *Romeo and Juliet* where both lovers kill themselves because they can't live without each other. But the mechanicals get everything wrong, and their attempts at tragedy produces tears of laughter, not of sadness!

One volunteer pupil acts as the 'dead' Pyramus. Make sure every pupil can see Pyramus (who might slump in a chair or lie on a table). Ask the class what they think the atmosphere would be like at the end of a play in which two young lovers kill themselves. After their suggestions, say 'Well, listen to this', and go to town with your performance of Thisbe! Some hints:

- Over-act Thisbe's entrance and her first sight of Pyramus (joy?).
- What does she do when she discovers Pyramus is dead, not asleep? Make the discovery as funny as you can.
- On 'eyes', 'lips', 'nose' and 'cheeks' point to those features on Pyramus' or your own face. Emphasise the descriptions 'lily lips', 'cherry nose', 'yellow cowslip cheeks', and 'His eyes were green as leeks'. It adds to the humour if you speak all the absurd comparisons absolutely seriously, as if you really meant them.
- Exaggerate your gestures on 'shore With shears his thread of silk'. This gives pupils a first visual impression of the ' thread and thrum' of human life being cut (see Bottom's speech on page 30). Don't explain 'sisters three' until you have completed the speech.
- Thisbe's farewell and suicide is an invitation to imaginative invention. You might repeat 'farewell friends' several times to different groups in the class. Make each 'adieu' a surprise, as your Thisbe recovers from apparent death to bid yet another farewell.
- To alert pupils to the rhyme scheme, show the problems you have in trying to rhyme 'tomb' with 'dumb', and 'word' with 'sword'.

Group work

Students work in pairs, taking turns to be Thisbe and Pyramus.

Independent work

Use any worksheet from pages 96–107.

OR

Invent six lines imitating 'These lily lips …' to '… green as leeks.'

A Midsummer Night's Dream
Farewell to the audience

If we shadows have offended,
Think but this, and all is mended:
That you have but slumbered here
While these visions did appear;
And this weak and idle theme,
No more yielding but a dream.
Gentles, do not reprehend,
If you pardon, we will mend.
And, as I am an honest Puck,
If we have unearnèd luck
Now to 'scape the serpent's tongue
We will make amends ere long,
Else the Puck a liar call.
So, good night unto you all.
Give me your hands, if we be friends,
And Robin shall restore amends.

STORY

Puck asks the audience to think of the play as a dream, and so forgive any offence the actors have caused. To avoid the audience hissing them, the actors will do better in the future. Puck calls for applause.

CHARACTERS

PUCK a spirit who attends on Oberon, King of the Fairies

LANGUAGE

shadows actors
weak and idle theme
    unimportant play
No more yielding
    offering no more
Gentles ladies and gentlemen
reprehend rebuke, find fault
'scape the serpent's tongue
    escape hisses from the audience

Puck's epilogue, with its strong rhyming couplets makes a delightful conclusion to A Midsummer Night's Dream *(and to your pupils' work on any Shakespeare play). It also provides the opportunity to show how the grave accent in 'unearnèd', and the changing of 'escape' to ''scape', maintains the rhythm of the verse.*

TEACHING SUGGESTIONS

Whole class

This is an epilogue: a speech spoken at the end of a play. It acknowledges the bond between actors and audience, and creates a feeling of togetherness in which the audience can show, with their applause, how much they have enjoyed the performance. On stage, Puck's epilogue is spoken by a single actor. But it offers excellent opportunities for choral speaking in which every pupil can share the language, and add actions.

Speak the lines a couplet (two lines) at a time with the class repeating after you. Ask for suggestions of what actions might accompany each couplet to illustrate the language. For example, couplet by couplet:

- 'we shadows' – all the actors bow, or strike a pose.
- 'these visions' – an opportunity for pairs of pupils to mime a few episodes from the play: Egeus raging at his daughter; Titania and Oberon quarrelling; Bottom and Flute whispering as Pyramus and Thisbe, etc.
- 'No more yielding but a dream' – pupils sigh, spread their arms to show how empty it all is, and close their eyes in contented sleep.
- 'reprehend' – shake finger disapprovingly.
- 'unearnèd luck' – spin a coin? fingers crossed?
- 'serpent's tongue' – everyone hisses to show displeasure.
- 'a liar call' – hands on heart, looking in wide-eyed innocence.
- 'hands' – stretch out hands, begin to clap.

Ask the pupils how they would take the curtain call. Each individual could take a bow in a different way to suggest a typical gesture of 'their' character. Remind the class that actors rehearse their curtain call very carefully to ensure that the final view the audience sees of the actors is that of a team working together.

Group work

Small groups rehearse their versions of the epilogue, working out how the lines can be shared between all pupils.

Independent work

Use any worksheet from pages 96–107.

OR

Write an epilogue that includes the names of everyone in your group.

Macbeth
Meet the characters

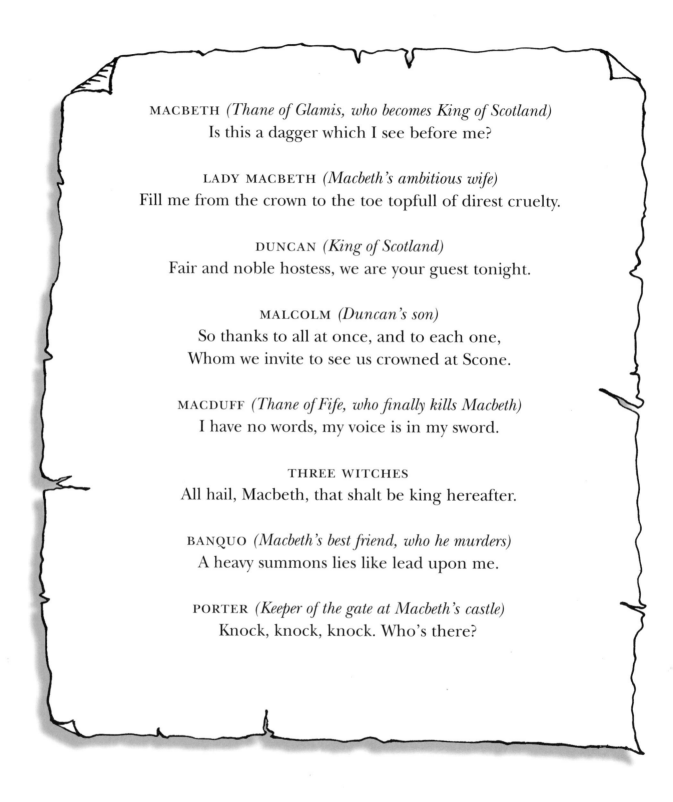

MACBETH *(Thane of Glamis, who becomes King of Scotland)*
Is this a dagger which I see before me?

LADY MACBETH *(Macbeth's ambitious wife)*
Fill me from the crown to the toe topfull of direst cruelty.

DUNCAN *(King of Scotland)*
Fair and noble hostess, we are your guest tonight.

MALCOLM *(Duncan's son)*
So thanks to all at once, and to each one,
Whom we invite to see us crowned at Scone.

MACDUFF *(Thane of Fife, who finally kills Macbeth)*
I have no words, my voice is in my sword.

THREE WITCHES
All hail, Macbeth, that shalt be king hereafter.

BANQUO *(Macbeth's best friend, who he murders)*
A heavy summons lies like lead upon me.

PORTER *(Keeper of the gate at Macbeth's castle)*
Knock, knock, knock. Who's there?

Macbeth Meet the characters

STORY

This introductory lesson on characters enables pupils to explore and hypothesise what the story of the play might be.

CHARACTERS

As named on the pupils' script.

LANGUAGE

Thane nobleman of Scotland
Glamis
   (usually pronounced Glams)
crown head
direst most dreadful
Scone
   (usually pronounced Scoon)
hereafter in the future

This lesson uses active methods to introduce major characters in the play. It helps pupils discover how Shakespeare creates character through language, and it enables them to speculate about what the characters are like, how they interact and how the story might develop.

TEACHING SUGGESTIONS

Whole class

Tell the class that they are going to get acquainted with some of the characters in *Macbeth* – and find out what they are like! Take each character in turn. Give pupils the name and brief description on the script, and speak their language. Pupils speak the line after you and strike a pose ('statue' or 'tableau') to portray the character who speaks. The portrayals can be done with pupils out of their seats, or sitting down if you prefer.

Don't be afraid to give pupils all kinds of prompts. What sort of person is Lady Macbeth who wants to be filled from head to feet with the most dreadful cruelty? Or Duncan, who greets her as 'Fair and noble hostess'?

Invite pupils to look at each others' 'statues' (this develops ideas about different ways of portrayal). Encourage class discussion of each character, asking pupils to give reasons for the sort of person they portray. Give the pupils plenty of practice, and use some of these active guessing 'games':

- Choose a character (without telling the class). Strike a pose, without speaking – pupils guess which character is portrayed, and the language spoken.
- Speak a line – pupils name the character.
- Describe a character, e.g. 'Thane of Fife' – pupils name the character.
- Name a character – pupils speak the character's line, and strike a pose.
- Choose two characters and set up a tableau to show them in relation to each other – for example, how might Macbeth and Banquo behave together?
- Invite pupils to create their own story – what sort of play has these characters in it?

Group work

Pairs or small groups work through their scripts, trying out poses and speaking the language. They play the 'guess the character' activities above.

Independent work

Use the language to make up your own story of what happens in the play.

OR

Choose one character. Write what you think happens to him or her in the play.

Macbeth
Macbeth in ten actions!

All hail, Macbeth, that shalt be king hereafter.

Look like the innocent flower, but be the serpent under it.

Is this a dagger which I see before me?

O, horror, horror, horror!

O, full of scorpions is my mind, dear wife!

O, treachery!

Avaunt and quit my sight!

Out damned spot! Out, I say!

Lay on, Macduff!

Hail, King of Scotland!

Macbeth Macbeth in ten actions!

STORY

An opportunity for pupils to act out the whole play in ten actions!

CHARACTERS

As introduced in Teaching suggestions (right).

LANGUAGE

Avaunt clear off!
spot drop of blood
Lay on prepare to fight

This is a lively and enjoyable introduction to the play. The vivid language from ten memorable moments in Macbeth *gives pupils active opportunities to play major characters and to acquire a sense of the structure of the play from beginning to end.*

Using frequent dramatic pauses, the teacher narrates the story (as in Teaching suggestions, right), and speaks the lines, adding actions and expressions to help pupils' own speaking and actions. After each line, pupils, in pairs, step into role, repeat the line, and act it out.

TEACHING SUGGESTIONS

Whole class

Add to the following teacher commentary as you wish:

1   Macbeth, a mighty warrior, is greeted by three witches. They prophesy a great future for him: 'All hail, Macbeth, that shalt be king hereafter.' (Pupils speak and enact as witches.)

2   So Macbeth thinks he will become King of Scotland. But there already is a king – Duncan! Macbeth's wife urges him to welcome Duncan, but to kill him when he sleeps: 'Look like the innocent flower, but be the serpent under it.' (Pupils speak and enact as Lady Macbeth and Macbeth.)

3   Macbeth agrees to do the murder – but he sees a supernatural dagger appear: 'Is this a dagger which I see before me?' (Pupils speak and enact as Macbeth.)

4   Macbeth kills Duncan. When the deed is discovered everyone cries out in horror: 'O, horror, horror, horror!' (Pupils speak and enact the line.}

5   Macbeth becomes king – but is troubled by his guilty conscience: 'O, full of scorpions is my mind, dear wife!' (Pupils speak and enact as Macbeth, e.g. holding head – scorpions really sting!)

6   Macbeth decides to kill everyone who may be a danger to him. His murderers assassinate his best friend, Banquo, who, as he is killed, suspects Macbeth's treachery: 'O, treachery!' (Pupils speak and enact the murder.)

7   Macbeth holds a splendid banquet – but the ghost of Banquo appears! Macbeth orders it away: 'Avaunt and quit my sight!' (Pupils speak and enact, as Macbeth and Banquo's Ghost.)

8   Things get worse. Macbeth's wife has terrible dreams. She sleepwalks, trying to rub the blood of Macbeth's victims off her hands: 'Out damned spot! Out, I say!' (Pupils speak and enact.)

9   At last Macbeth is trapped! His greatest enemy Macduff challenges him to a final sword fight. Macbeth accepts the challenge: 'Lay on, Macduff!' – but is killed (Pupils speak and enact. Use a 'freeze' of fight to ensure you maintain control.)

10 Order is restored to Scotland. Everyone greets Duncan's son Malcolm as the rightful king: 'Hail, King of Scotland!' (Pupils speak and enact.)

Group work

In pairs or small groups, pupils rehearse and present 'the whole play'.

Independent work

Write the story of Macbeth. Include all the language you have learned.

Macbeth
Meet the witches!

FIRST WITCH	When shall we three meet again?
	In thunder, lightning or in rain?
SECOND WITCH	When the hurly-burly's done,
	When the battle's lost, and won.
THIRD WITCH	That will be ere the set of sun.
FIRST WITCH	Where the place?
SECOND WITCH	Upon the heath.
THIRD WITCH	There to meet with Macbeth.
FIRST WITCH	I come, Graymalkin.
SECOND WITCH	Paddock calls.
THIRD WITCH	Anon.
ALL WITCHES	Fair is foul and foul is fair,
	Hover through the fog and filthy air.

Macbeth Meet the witches!

STORY

The three witches prepare for their meeting with Macbeth, whose army is fighting a mighty battle against King Duncan's enemies.

CHARACTERS

FIRST WITCH
SECOND WITCH
THIRD WITCH

LANGUAGE

hurly-burly fighting, commotion
ere before
Graymalkin, Paddock
  grey cat, toad (the witches' 'familiars'). Witches were believed to have 'familiar spirits', demons who helped them with their evil work. The familiars were usually animals or birds.

The rhythm of the lines is a great help to pupils. It is the well known 'four-beat' pattern of nursery rhymes, spell-like and incantatory: de-dum de-dum de-dum de-dum. Pupils respond to the rhythm instinctively, chanting the opening and closing lines.

TEACHING SUGGESTIONS

Whole class

You can make your introduction as long or as short as you wish, depending on what you know your class enjoys. The basic situation is set out in the Story (see left), but you can embroider as much as you and the pupils like. But it is helpful to remember that Shakespeare simply pitches the audience straight into this opening scene of the play without warning or preparation, inviting them to make up their own minds about what's going on.

Take the whole class through the scene, a short section at a time. Speak the lines, with the class repeating them after you. Make your delivery as exciting as possible, and use a different 'voice' for each witch. Emphasise the four-beat rhythm of the first four and last two lines.

Briefly explain words like 'hurly-burly' and 'ere' as they occur. You will find that some pupils in the class will be able to respond if you ask them to 'show me a hurly-burly'. Use the explanation of 'familiars' (left) to help pupils' understanding of 'Graymalkin' and 'Paddock'.

When the whole class has spoken the scene, invite the pupils to brainstorm the following questions to help them form ideas of what the witches are like:

- What do the witches wear?
- How do they move?
- How is each witch different from the other?
- How does each witch speak?
- What gestures and expressions do they use?
- What sound effects could you add?
- What do you think the witches will do when they meet Macbeth?

Group work

The task for each group is an exciting challenge: how can you stage this opening scene of the play to greatest dramatic effect – to really scare the audience? Pupils work in threes, but larger groups are also appropriate in which each pupil contributes in some way to the presentation (for example, adding sound effects, or as the 'familiars').

Independent work

Use any worksheet from pages 96–107.

OR

Invent a 'familiar' (creature and sound) for the Third Witch, and write about what the witches intend to do when they meet Macbeth.

Macbeth
The witches predict the future

ALL WITCHES	The weird sisters, hand in hand,
	Posters of the sea and land,
	Thus do go, about, about,
	Thrice to thine, and thrice to mine,
	And thrice again, to make up nine.
	Peace, the charm's wound up.

Enter MACBETH *and* BANQUO.

MACBETH	So foul and fair a day I have not seen.
BANQUO	What are these,
	So withered and so wild in their attire?
MACBETH	Speak if you can. What are you?
FIRST WITCH	All hail Macbeth, hail to thee, Thane of Glamis.
SECOND WITCH	All hail Macbeth, hail to thee, Thane of Cawdor.
THIRD WITCH	All hail Macbeth, that shall be king hereafter.
BANQUO	If you can look into the seeds of time,
	And say which grain will grow and which will not,
	Speak then to me.

FIRST WITCH	Hail.
SECOND WITCH	Hail.
THIRD WITCH	Hail.

FIRST WITCH	Lesser than Macbeth, and greater.
SECOND WITCH	Not so happy, yet much happier.
THIRD WITCH	Thou shalt get kings, though thou be none.
ALL	So all hail Macbeth and Banquo.
MACBETH	Stay, you imperfect speakers. Tell me why
	Upon this blasted heath you stop our way.

The witches vanish. Macbeth and Banquo look amazed.

Stepping into Shakespeare © Cambridge University Press 2000. See notice on p. ii

Macbeth The witches predict the future

STORY

The witches greet Macbeth, predicting that he will become king. Banquo asks to know his future, but the witches give him puzzling replies.

CHARACTERS

FIRST WITCH
SECOND WITCH
THIRD WITCH
MACBETH and BANQUO
    Thanes (noblemen of
    Scotland), leaders of King
    Duncan's army

LANGUAGE

weird sisters
    in Shakespeare's time this did
    not simply mean 'strange or
    peculiar women', but meant
    goddesses of destiny who
    could predict the future
Posters fast travellers
the charm the spell
Thane of Glamis, Thane of
    Cawdor titles of high ranking
    Scottish noblemen ('Glamis' is
    often pronounced as 'Glams')
hereafter in the future
Thou shalt get kings
    you will be the father of kings

*The witches' language is
powerfully rhythmical: sing-song,
repetitive, hypnotic. Banquo's
vivid image 'look into the seeds
of time' can inspire pupils'
imaginative writing.*

TEACHING SUGGESTIONS

Whole class

Call for three volunteers to be the three witches. Ask the class how they think the witches would move as they speak their first six lines, and say 'Let's see if Shakespeare gives us a clue in the language.'

Then speak the lines to emphasise the sing-song, rhythmical effect. Invite the class to contribute ideas that the three volunteers can try out. Make sure the pupils' contributions include what the witches might do on 'Thrice to thine', etc.: what action could they perform three times ('thrice')? End this part of the lesson with the whole class speaking the six lines together as the volunteers move.

Next, call for two more volunteers to act as Macbeth and Banquo. Ask the class for suggestions of how they enter (they are two warriors who have just won a great battle against King Duncan's enemies). Work through the witches' greetings, speaking each line to give the pupils an impression of the repetitive pattern and rhythm. Use different actions to accompany each repetition of 'Hail'.

Most pupils will probably not know what a 'Thane' is, so quickly explain and invite parallel examples, real or imagined ('Duke of Edinburgh', 'Lord of Loopyland', etc.).

Ask for suggestions about how the scene might end. How do the witches vanish, and how do Banquo and Macbeth react? Macbeth is already Thane of Glamis, but he is surprised to hear himself called Thane of Cawdor because he believes the Thane of Cawdor is still alive. He is probably even more astounded to be hailed as a future king.

Group work

Students work in groups of five (or more by adding in a narrator or director role). Each group's task is to work out a thrilling presentation of the scene. Provide reminders of some of the points which have emerged from whole class work, e.g. how the witches speak their spell to wind up 'the charm'; how the scene ends (is Macbeth friendly towards Banquo after hearing the witches' predictions?).

Independent work

Use any worksheet from pages 96–107.

OR

Write Macbeth's letter to his wife telling of the meeting with the witches and his thoughts about Banquo.

Macbeth   Lady Macbeth plots Duncan's murder

LADY MACBETH   The raven himself is hoarse,
That croaks the fatal entrance of Duncan
Under my battlements. Come, you spirits,
You murdering ministers, who wait on nature's mischief,
Fill me from the crown to the toe topfull
Of direst cruelty. Come, thick night,
And pall thee in the dunnest smoke of hell,
That my keen knife sees not the wound it makes.

The spirits dance and echo her words. Enter MACBETH.

MACBETH   My dearest love, Duncan comes here tonight.
LADY MACBETH   And when goes hence?
MACBETH   Tomorrow as he purposes.
LADY MACBETH   O never shall sun that morrow see.
Look like the innocent flower, but be the serpent under it.
He that's coming must be provided for.
Leave all the rest to me   *Exit Macbeth.*

Enter KING DUNCAN *and his court to greet Lady Macbeth.*

DUNCAN   Our honoured hostess. Where's the Thane of Cawdor?
Give me your hand, conduct me to mine host.
We love him highly. We are your guest tonight.

Lady Macbeth shows welcome. She leads Duncan off stage.

Stepping into Shakespeare © Cambridge University Press 2000. See notice on p. ii

Macbeth Lady Macbeth plots Duncan's murder

STORY

Lady Macbeth calls on evil spirits to help her murder King Duncan. She tells Macbeth that she will arrange the murder. She greets Duncan as a welcome guest.

CHARACTERS

LADY MACBETH
EVIL SPIRITS
MACBETH
KING DUNCAN
COURTIERS attendants on the king

LANGUAGE

crown head
direst most dreadful
pall thee in the dunnest smoke
   hide you in the darkest clouds
keen sharp
provided for prepared for (killed)

Shakespeare's language gives you the opportunity to create three very different moods in the scene:

- *the evil atmosphere of Lady Macbeth's wicked prayer to her spirits.*
- *an ominous mood, as she advises Macbeth to behave deceitfully.*
- *an atmosphere of false welcome as she hides her ill intentions, responding to Duncan's kind words.*

TEACHING SUGGESTIONS

Whole class

Set the scene. Macbeth has written to his wife telling of the witches' prophecy that he will be king. The news awakes evil in Lady Macbeth. She plans to murder King Duncan who is even now approaching her castle, intending to feast and sleep there.

Invite four or five volunteers to act as Lady Macbeth and her evil spirits. Her opening speech is a kind of wicked prayer, asking evil spirits to help her carry out the murder. Take the three sentences one at a time, asking the class for suggestions of how Lady Macbeth and her spirits might speak and behave. Possible questions include: What sound does a raven make? How might the spirits mime Duncan's 'fatal entrance' to the castle, to show what will happen to him? The spirits 'wait on (attend, serve) nature's mischief' – what might those 'mischiefs' be? Which words might the spirits echo?

After class discussion, speak the eight lines in short sections, with the class repeating each section, and the volunteers miming. Heavily emphasise the two commands: 'Come', 'Come'.

Speak Lady Macbeth's conversation with her husband to give the class a general sense of what is happening. Invite ideas how to stage the episode. Does Macbeth suspect her murderous intentions from the start? Does he leave fearfully, or is he happy about the plan? Does she order him about? Does he try to protest?

Spend some time on the image 'Look like the innocent flower, but be the serpent under it.' Ask the pupils what picture it conjures up in their minds, and invite volunteer pairs to show a tableau (living statue) of it to the whole class.

More volunteers can enact pupils' suggestions of how to stage the third part of the scene: King Duncan's entrance. How would a King of Scotland enter the castle of a man he thinks to be a loyal friend? Which of Duncan's words show that his mood is friendship and hospitality? How might Lady Macbeth lead Duncan off in a way that he thinks is friendly, but the audience knows is deceitful?

Group work

Pupils work in groups of six or more. They first prepare a tableau of 'Look like the innocent flower, but be the serpent under it.' They then work out their version of the whole scene.

Independent work

Use any worksheet from pages 96–107.

OR

Write Lady Macbeth's diary entry of what she did today.

Macbeth
Macbeth sees the dagger

Is this a dagger which I see before me,
The handle toward my hand? Come, let me clutch thee.
I have thee not, and yet I see thee still.
Art thou not, fatal vision, sensible
To feeling as to sight? Or art thou but
A dagger of the mind, a false creation,
Proceeding from the heat-oppressèd brain?
I see thee yet, in form as palpable
As this which now I draw.
I see thee still, and on thy blade and dudgeon
Gouts of blood, which was not so before.
There's no such thing!
                    Now o'er the one half-world
Nature seems dead, and withered murder,
Alarumed by his sentinel, the wolf,
Thus with his stealthy pace, moves like a ghost.
Thou sure and firm-set earth, hear not my steps,
For fear thy very stones prate of my whereabouts,
And take the present horror from the time.   (*A bell rings*)
I go, and it is done. The bell invites me.
Hear it not, Duncan, for it is a knell
That summons thee to heaven or to hell.

Macbeth Macbeth sees the dagger

Stepping into Shakespeare © Cambridge University Press 2000. See notice on p. ii

STORY

Lady Macbeth has persuaded Macbeth to kill King Duncan. Alone, in the courtyard of the castle, Macbeth hallucinates, thinking he sees an invisible dagger that invites him to do the murder.

CHARACTERS

MACBETH

LANGUAGE

fatal vision deadly sight
sensible to feeling
   able to be touched
heat-oppressèd
   feverish (Macbeth feels his brains are boiling)
palpable real, obvious, touchable
dudgeon handle
gouts large drops
one half-world night-time world
prate chatter
knell funeral bell

Macbeth's language is very physical, inviting pupils to perform actions and gestures as they speak. There is a memorable personification in 'withered murder'. The speech is a soliloquy (spoken by an actor alone on stage).

TEACHING SUGGESTIONS

Whole class

Remind the class of the situation. Macbeth did not want to kill King Duncan, but his wife mocked and bullied him into agreeing to do the murder. Now it is after midnight, and Macbeth is alone in the courtyard of his castle, trying to pluck up courage to go to the bedroom where Duncan is sleeping. He sees a vision (it may be helpful to introduce the word 'hallucination').

Speak the lines in short sections, with all the pupils repeating your words and actions. Try to convey the nervous, taut atmosphere, and the turmoil in Macbeth's mind, suggested by the urgent questions, commands and statements, for example:

- 'Is this a dagger which I see before me' – start back with look of horror.
- 'The handle toward my hand?' – puzzled look, slight hand gesture.
- 'Come, let me clutch thee' – rapid seizing gesture.

Remember that for the first 12 lines Macbeth is speaking to the dagger. Pupils follow your example and fix their eyes on a space in front of them, and use appropriate facial expressions as Macbeth puzzles over what he is seeing, then finally dismisses it as an illusion with 'There's no such thing!'

The section 'Now o'er the one half-world … horror from the time.' is very atmospheric, and you can lower your voice almost to a fearful whisper which the pupils can repeat. The final three lines are full of determination.

After your demonstration, set the class the practical puzzle of how the soliloquy might be delivered if the witches are involved. Volunteers as Macbeth and the three witches can act out class suggestions on how the witches present the phantom dagger to Macbeth's eyes, and act out dead Nature, withered murder, and the wolf. They can also echo words identified by the class.

Group work

Each group of four or more pupils works out a performance of the soliloquy. Their task is to create an intense atmosphere of fear and menace. Give pupils the choice of whether or not to involve the witches in the speaking and action (e.g. in the final three lines the witches might ring the bell, gently take Macbeth by the hand, and lead him towards the sleeping Duncan).

Independent work

Use any worksheet from pages 96–107.

OR

Write your own poem imagining you see a phantom vision.
Begin with 'Is this a … which I see before me?'

Macbeth
Plotting Banquo's murder

MACBETH is crowned king in great ceremony. Then everyone leaves, except Macbeth. He takes off his crown and looks at it.

MACBETH   To be thus is nothing, but to be safely thus.
Our fears in Banquo stick deep. He chid the sisters
When first they put the name of king upon me.
They hailed him father to a line of kings.
For them, the gracious Duncan have I murdered,
To make them kings, the seed of Banquo kings.

Enter two MURDERERS.

MACBETH   Both of you know Banquo was your enemy.
MURDERERS   True, my lord.
MACBETH   So is he mine. (*Whispers in the Murderers' ears*) It must be done tonight.
Fleance, his son that keeps him company,
Must embrace the fate of that dark hour.
MURDERERS   We are resolved, my lord. (*They leave*)
MACBETH   Ere the bat has flown his cloistered flight,
There shall be done a deed of dreadful note.
Come seeling night,
Scarf up the tender eye of pitiful day.
Light thickens, and the crow makes wing to the rooky wood.
Good things of day begin to droop and drowse,
Whiles night's black agents to their preys do rouse.

STORY

Macbeth has killed King Duncan, and has thrown suspicion for the murder on Duncan's sons. Now he is crowned as king, but he feels uneasy about Banquo, because the witches had prophesied that Banquo's descendants would become kings. He plots Banquo's murder.

CHARACTERS

MACBETH
PEOPLE OF SCOTLAND
   who crown Macbeth as king
TWO MURDERERS

LANGUAGE

stick deep cut into me painfully
chid rebuked, criticised
sisters witches
   ('the weird sisters')
seed of Banquo
   Banquo's children
Ere before
cloistered flight
   flight around the cloisters
   (covered walkway in a
   monastery)
seeling
   blinding (hawks' eyes were
   'seeled' by sewing them up)
do rouse awake, begin hunting

The language and rhythms of Macbeth's opening and closing soliloquies convey a powerful sense of ominous menace. The scene contains many remarkable images which can fire pupils' imaginations.

TEACHING SUGGESTIONS

Whole class

The scene has four episodes:

1   The coronation of Macbeth. You may wish to spend a whole lesson on this. Pupils enjoy inventing their own ceremonies and language for the crowning of Macbeth.

2   Macbeth's first soliloquy. Macbeth fears that he is not secure as king, because the witches prophesied that Banquo's children would become kings. Ask the class how a person behaves when they are deeply worried about the future. Build their suggestions into how you speak each short section.

When you speak the first line, find ways of conveying to the class what 'thus' means (you could touch an imaginary crown, or take it off and look at it, then replace it on the second 'thus'). You may find it helpful to have an object in your hand (e.g. a pencil) to signify Banquo. Look at it, or perform some action with it, each time you mention Banquo or his descendants ('He', 'him', 'line of kings', 'them', 'seed of Banquo').

3   Planning the murder. Use two volunteers from the class, and ask the class for suggestions about how they enter and leave, what Macbeth whispers to them, and whether he is cold or friendly to them. The image 'Must embrace the fate of that dark hour.' is very powerful. Ask the pupils to show you, with a gesture, just what Macbeth means. Why doesn't he simply say 'Fleance must also be killed'?

4   Macbeth's prediction of the murder. In the final seven lines Macbeth predicts that Banquo will be killed before nightfall (bats come out at dusk). His lines are like an evil spell, full of foreboding images. You will need to explain 'seeling' (see left), but the language and rhythm can convey a powerful sense of threatening menace.

Group work

Large groups can work on the coronation episode. Groups of three or more can rehearse the three following episodes in which there are all kinds of practical decisions to be taken: does Macbeth stand or sit, move or stay still? What is his mood in each episode?

Independent work

Use any worksheet from pages 96–107.

OR

Learn the last seven lines by heart. Really scare your hearers as you speak them.

Macbeth
Banquo's ghost

Enter MACBETH *and* LADY MACBETH *as King and Queen,*
followed by the Thanes of Scotland.

MACBETH You know your own degrees, sit down.
At first and last, the hearty welcome.

The Banquet begins. Macbeth walks around greeting his guests.
The GHOST OF BANQUO *enters and sits in Macbeth's place.*
Macbeth sees the Ghost. It is invisible to everyone else.

MACBETH Which of you have done this? Thou canst not say I did it.
Never shake thy gory locks at me!
Prithee, see there! Behold, look, lo! How say you?

Exit Ghost of Banquo.

LADY MACBETH Sit, worthy friends. My lord is often thus.
He will again be well. Feed, and regard him not.
(*To Macbeth*) Are you a man?
This is the very painting of your fear.

MACBETH I do forget. Give me some wine, fill, fill!
I drink to the general joy of the whole table,
And to our dear friend Banquo, whom we miss.

Enter GHOST OF BANQUO. *Macbeth sees the Ghost.*

Avaunt and quit my sight! Let the earth hide thee!
Thy bones are marrowless, thy blood is cold.
Thou hast no speculation in those eyes
Which thou dost glare with.
Approach thou like the rugged Russian bear,
The armed rhinoceros, or the Hyrcan tiger,
Take any shape but that. Hence horrible shadow.
Unreal mockery hence.   (*Exit Ghost of Banquo*)

LADY MACBETH (*To lords*) I pray you speak not. At once, good night.
Stand not upon the order of your going,
But go at once.   (*All the lords leave*)

MACBETH It will have blood they say: blood will have blood.
I will tomorrow to the weird sisters,
For I am bent to know, by the worst means, the worst.
For mine own good, all causes shall give way.

Macbeth Banquo's ghost

STORY

Banquo has been murdered on Macbeth's orders. Macbeth now welcomes all the Thanes (noblemen) of Scotland to a magnificent banquet. But Banquo's ghost appears – with disturbing results! Macbeth resolves to visit the witches.

CHARACTERS

MACBETH King of Scotland
LADY MACBETH Queen of Scotland
BANQUO'S GHOST
THANES noblemen of Scotland

LANGUAGE

degrees social status (which determined where they sat at table)
gory locks bloodstained hair
Prithee I pray you (please)
Avaunt clear off!
speculation vision, ability to see
Hyrcan tiger savage tiger (from Hyrcania near the Caspian Sea)
Stand not upon the order of your going don't leave in order of rank (normally the highest ranking would leave first)
weird sisters witches
bent determined
worst means most evil messengers (the witches)
all causes everybody else's wishes

Macbeth's language as he tries to order the ghost away ('Avaunt ... hence') is full of short commands and statements that pupils enjoy speaking to each other.

TEACHING SUGGESTIONS

Whole class

Discuss with the class how to stage the scene in the classroom. A few chairs (one as a throne) set out at the front of the room can work well. Ask for ideas about how a king and queen might enter. Pupil volunteers can put some of the suggestions into practice and act as thanes.

A herald might announce each thane as they enter (make up names and titles). Macbeth's command that they sit in order of their social status can have comic results as the thanes sort themselves out, the most important sitting nearest the throne.

Speak the scene a short section at a time, with pupils repeating your words and actions. Remind the class that only Macbeth can see the ghost, and that on stage the scene should be full of suspense, keeping the audience on the edge of their seats. Ask for suggestions on how to stage the ghost's two appearances to greatest dramatic effect:

- How might the ghost enter?
- What does it do before sitting in Macbeth's place?
- How does Macbeth react?
- How does Macbeth speak each short section, trying to order the ghost away?
- How do the thanes react to the sight of their king raving like a madman?
- What does the ghost do in response to Macbeth's words? How does it exit?
- How do the thanes leave in response to Lady Macbeth's command?
- When only Macbeth and Lady Macbeth are left on stage, how do they behave towards each other, and how does Macbeth speak his final four lines?

Group work

The class can divide into two large groups to prepare performances of the scene. Pupils can also work successfully in much smaller groups with only one or two thanes.

Independent work

Use any worksheet from pages 96–107.

OR

Step into role as a thane. Write your account of what you saw at the banquet.

Macbeth
The witches prepare their cauldron

FIRST WITCH	Thrice the brindled cat hath mewed.
SECOND WITCH	Thrice and once the hedge-pig whined.
THIRD WITCH	Harpier cries, 'Tis time, 'tis time!
FIRST WITCH	Round about the cauldron go,
	In the poisoned entrails throw.
	Toad, that under cold stone
	Days and night has thirty-one.
	Sweltered venom sleeping got,
	Boil thou first in the charmèd pot.
ALL	Double, double, toil and trouble,
	Fire burn, and cauldron bubble.
SECOND WITCH	Fillet of a fenny snake,
	In the cauldron boil and bake.
	Eye of newt, and toe of frog,
	Wool of bat, and tongue of dog,
	Adder's fork, and blind-worm's sting,
	Lizard's leg and howlet's wing.
	For a charm of powerful trouble,
	Like a hell-broth, boil and bubble.
ALL	Double, double, toil and trouble,
	Fire burn, and cauldron bubble.
THIRD WITCH	Scale of dragon, tooth of wolf,
	Witches' mummy, maw and gulf
	Of the ravined salt-sea shark.
	Root of hemlock, digged in the dark.
	Add thereto a tiger's chaudron,
	For the ingredients of our cauldron.
SECOND WITCH	Cool it with a baboon's blood,
	Then the charm is firm and good.
ALL	Double, double, toil and trouble,
	Fire burn, and cauldron bubble.

Macbeth The witches prepare their cauldron

STORY

The witches are waiting for Macbeth to arrive, when they will reveal the future to him. They drop all kinds of horrible ingredients into their cauldron to prepare their magic brew.

CHARACTERS

FIRST WITCH
SECOND WITCH
THIRD WITCH

LANGUAGE

brindled streaked with colour
hedge-pig hedgehog
Harpier name of a witch's familiar
   (a harpy had a woman's face
   and a bird's body)
Sweltered venom
   poisonous sweat
fenny snake
   snake from a fen or marsh
Wool of bat bat's skin
Adder's fork
   snake's forked tongue
howlet young owl
mummy mummified corpse
maw and gulf
   stomach and gullet
ravined full of devoured prey
hemlock poisonous plant
chaudron entrails

The familiar four-beat rhythm (de-dum de-dum de-dum de-dum), and the list of exotic ingredients, hold great appeal for younger pupils, making the scene immediately accessible.

TEACHING SUGGESTIONS

Whole class

This is one of the most popular scenes of all in school Shakespeare. Younger pupils especially enjoy the hypnotic rhythm and rhyme as they chant the list of sickening ingredients. The outlandish vocabulary and the repeated refrain ('Double, double …') help pupils to create a strange, supernatural atmosphere.

The whole class element of this lesson can therefore be shorter than for most other scenes, but needs to include:

- All the pupils chanting all the lines together to gain a first sense of meaning and rhythm.
- Working in three large groups, with each group speaking as one of the witches (the whole class speak the 'chorus' together: 'Double, double, …').
- Pupil discussion, pooling ideas on how the witches might move and speak.
- Brief explanations by the teacher of 'Harpier' (see left, and information on witches' familiars on page 41), and other unfamiliar words. Pupils may well know or guess some words, and you can help them with your actions as you speak each line for them to repeat after you. For example, pat your stomach and indicate your gullet on 'maw and gulf'.
- Brief explanation of how the grave accent ('charmèd') helps to maintain the four-beat rhythm.

Group work

Pupils work in groups of three or more to prepare a performance (large groups can work well, with pupils speaking in unison). Different pupils may speak alternate lines throughout, or several pupils might join in speaking the same line as well as joining in the 'chorus'. Each group will find a method it prefers.

Independent work

Use any worksheet from pages 96–107.

OR

Pupils write their own list of ingredients, copying Shakespeare's rhythm and rhyme scheme. It is easiest to start with the four lines beginning 'Eye of newt, and toe of frog', because pupils can make direct substitutions for each of the nouns. Pupils might also invent a different 'chorus'.

Macbeth
Macbeth sees the apparitions

MACBETH
How now, you secret, black and midnight hags!
I conjure you by that which you profess,
Howe'er you come to know it, answer me.

ALL WITCHES
Speak. Demand. We'll answer.
Come high or low, thyself and office deftly show.

Thunder. Enter FIRST APPARITION, *an armed head.*

FIRST APPARITION
Macbeth, Macbeth, Macbeth. Beware Macduff,
Beware the Thane of Fife. Dismiss me. Enough. (*Vanishes*)

Thunder. Enter SECOND APPARITION, *a bloody child.*

SECOND APPARITION
Macbeth, Macbeth, Macbeth.
Be bloody, bold, and resolute. Laugh to scorn
The power of man, for none of woman born
Shall harm Macbeth. (*Vanishes*)

Thunder. Enter THIRD APPARITION, *a child crowned,*
with a tree in his hand.

THIRD APPARITION
Be lion-mettled, proud, and take no care.
Macbeth shall never vanquished be, until
Great Birnam Wood shall come to Dunsinane. (*Vanishes*)

MACBETH
That will never be. Tell me,
Shall Banquo's issue ever reign in this kingdom?

ALL WITCHES
Seek to know no more.

MACBETH
Deny me this and an eternal curse fall on you.

ALL WITCHES
Show! Show! Show!
Show his eyes and grieve his heart,
Come like shadows, so depart.

Enter a show of eight kings. The last king carries a glass in his
hand – Banquo's Ghost following.

MACBETH
Filthy hags, why do you show me this?
What, will the line stretch out to the crack of doom?
I'll see no more. Horrible sight!
The blood-boltered Banquo smiles upon me.

Music. The witches dance and vanish, Macbeth is awestruck.

Macbeth Macbeth sees the apparitions

STORY

Macbeth visits the witches to discover what they predict for the future. The witches conjure up three apparitions (phantoms). They warn Macbeth against Macduff, and predict he cannot be killed by a naturally-born man, or until Birnam Wood comes to Dunsinane. Macbeth asks if Banquo's children will ever rule Scotland. The witches show him a line of eight kings and Banquo. The sight makes Macbeth angry.

CHARACTERS

THREE WITCHES
MACBETH
THREE APPARITIONS
   an armed head, a bloody child,
   a child crowned
EIGHT KINGS
BANQUO'S GHOST

LANGUAGE

conjure you demand of you
profess are expert in
   (your magic art)
thyself and office deftly show
   you and your meaning skilfully
   show
apparition phantom
resolute determined
lion-mettled brave as a lion
issue children, descendants
blood-boltered
   blood covered, hair matted
   with blood

The scene is full of urgent commands and spectacular appearances.

TEACHING SUGGESTIONS

Whole class

Tell the background in your own words, and use pupil volunteers to act out each episode in the scene. To help pupils gain a first impression, speak the lines with the whole class repeating after you. Give brief explanations in context. Afterwards, encourage pupil discussion on the following:

- Macbeth is visiting the witches to find out what the future holds in store for him. What atmosphere can the witches create before Macbeth speaks?

- Macbeth demands to know the future. Is he angry, or afraid, or … ?

- The witches conjure up (make appear) three apparitions. Can the pupils guess what an 'apparition' is (a phantom, ghost or magical appearance), and what each might mean for Macbeth's future? How might they present each apparition?

- 'an armed head': the head wearing a warlike helmet is a warning about Macduff ('the Thane of Fife') who will come in armour to slay Macbeth.

- 'a bloody child': the child covered in blood also portrays Macduff. The blood signifies that Macduff had a difficult birth ('none of woman born').

- 'a child crowned, with a tree in his hand': the third apparition probably portrays Banquo's son, who will become king. The 'tree' he carries signifies Birnam Wood, a forest about ten miles from Macbeth's castle at Dunsinane. But the tree might also signify the 'family tree' of all the kings who will descend from Banquo – a sight which appears as 'a show of eight kings'.

- The 'glass' which the last king carries is a mirror. There is a theatrical story that when Shakespeare's company performed before King James I, the mirror was held up so that King James could see his own reflection, and so think that he was also descended from Banquo. In fact, the Banquo 'family tree' is a complete invention. You could tell the pupils that Shakespeare found the idea in the history books he read, but those books often made things up.

Group work

Either divide the class into two large groups, and each group enacts the whole scene. Or have five smaller groups and give each a short unit (witches and Macbeth; First Apparition; Second Apparition; Third Apparition; show of eight kings). Each group prepares their episode, building up a whole class presentation.

Independent work

Use any worksheet from pages 96–107.

OR

Write one witch's story of preparing the apparitions for Macbeth's visit.

Macbeth
Lady Macbeth sleepwalks

Enter LADY MACBETH, *rubbing her hands.*

Yet here's a spot. Out damned spot! Out, I say!
One, two. Why, then 'tis time to do it. Hell is murky.
Fie my lord, fie, a soldier, and afeared? What need we fear?
Who knows it, when none can call our power to account?
Yet who would have thought the old man to have had so
much blood in him?

The Thane of Fife had a wife. Where is she now?
What, will these hands ne'er be clean?
No more of that, my lord, no more of that. You mar all with
this starting.

Here's the smell of the blood still.
All the perfumes of Arabia will not sweeten this little hand.
O, O, O.

Wash your hands, put on your night-gown, look not so pale.
I tell you yet again, Banquo's buried. He cannot come out
of his grave.

To bed, to bed. There's knocking at the gate.
Come, come, come, come, give me your hand.
What's done cannot be undone. To bed, to bed, to bed.

Macbeth Lady Macbeth sleepwalks

STORY

Lady Macbeth has helped her husband become King of Scotland. She forced him to murder King Duncan and seize the throne, and has watched him kill his enemies. Now she suffers from terrible nightmares, and as she sleepwalks, she remembers past murders.

CHARACTERS

LADY MACBETH
Others who might appear to act out Lady Macbeth's nightmares are King Duncan, Lady Macduff and her children, Banquo, the witches, Macbeth

LANGUAGE

spot spot of blood
murky dark, gloomy
Fie shame on you
call our power to account
   hold us responsible for our
   actions
Thane of Fife Macduff
mar all spoil everything
starting nervousness, jumpiness

Lady Macbeth's sleepwalking language is dreamlike: short and disjointed recollections of Macbeth's evil deeds. There are 26 sentences, each of which pupils can present as an action of some kind.

TEACHING SUGGESTIONS

Whole class

Begin with a class discussion on dreams and nightmares. What are they like? Do they flow as a series of smooth pictures, or do they jump about, with all kinds of improbable things happening? How do sleepwalkers move? If someone has done something very bad, does it return to haunt them when they sleep?

Write up some of the words to describe dreams suggested by the class (e.g. 'jerky', 'disconnected', 'jumpy', 'guilty', 'fearful'). Then speak the scene a short section at a time, with the class repeating your words and actions.

Lady Macbeth's language probably refers to:

- 'spot' – after Macbeth murdered the sleeping Duncan, Lady Macbeth's hands were covered in blood from the daggers.
- 'One, two' – Lady Macbeth struck a bell to tell her husband when it was 'time to do it' (murder Duncan).
- 'Fie my lord, fie, a soldier, and afeared?' – she accused Macbeth of cowardice, when he suffered agonies of guilt after the murder.
- 'none can call our power to account?' – she had assured Macbeth that no one will dare to accuse them of the murder.
- 'the old man' – Lady Macbeth almost killed Duncan herself, but suddenly thought that he resembled her own father.
- 'The Thane of Fife had a wife.' – Macbeth ordered the murder of Lady Macduff (wife of the Thane of Fife) and everyone at Macduff's castle.
- 'You mar all with this starting.' – Macbeth showed guilt and hesitation after committing the murder of Duncan.
- 'Banquo's buried.' – another of Macbeth's victims!
- 'There's knocking at the gate.' – after Duncan's murder, Macduff had hammered on the gate of Macbeth's castle.
- 'What's done cannot be undone.' – can pupils give examples of this from their own experience?

Group work

Act out her dreams! Groups of five or six work on the script. One pupil speaks the lines and the others enact the dream-pictures in Lady Macbeth's head.

Independent work

Use any worksheet from pages 96–107.

OR

Write the dream of someone whose crimes come back to haunt them.

Macbeth
The final battle

SIWARD	What wood is this before us?
MENTEITH	The wood of Birnam.
MALCOLM	Let every soldier hew him down a bough
	And bear it before him. Advance the war!

They march on the castle. MACBETH *sees them approaching.*

MACBETH	'Fear not, till Birnam Wood do come to Dunsinane',
	And now a wood comes towards Dunsinane.
	Arm, arm, and out!
	Ring the alarm bell! Blow wind, come wrack,
	At least we'll die with harness on our back.
MACDUFF	Make all our trumpets speak, give them all breath,
	Those clamorous harbingers of blood and death.

A battle in which Macbeth kills several soldiers,
then Macduff finds him.

MACDUFF	Tyrant, show thy face! Turn, hell-hound, turn!
MACBETH	Of all men else I have avoided thee.
	But get thee back, my soul is too much charged
	With blood of thine already.
MACDUFF	I have no words. My voice is in my sword.
MACBETH	I bear a charmèd life. I'll not fight with thee.
MACDUFF	Then yield thee coward.
MACBETH	I will not yield.
	Though Birnam Wood be come to Dunsinane,
	Yet I will try the last. Lay on, Macduff!

They fight and Macduff slays Macbeth. Enter MALCOLM.

MACDUFF	Hail, King of Scotland! The time is free!
	Behold where stands the usurper's cursed head.
ALL	Hail, King of Scotland!
MALCOLM	So, thanks to all at once, and to each one,
	Whom we invite to see us crowned at Scone.

A grand procession ending in Malcolm crowned as king.

Stepping into Shakespeare © Cambridge University Press 2000. See notice on p. ii

Macbeth The final battle

Prince Malcolm, son of the murdered King Duncan, leads an army against Macbeth. Using branches from Birnam Wood as camouflage, they attack Dunsinane Castle. Macbeth resists bravely but is slain by Macduff. Malcolm is proclaimed King of Scotland.

CHARACTERS

MALCOLM son of King Duncan
MACDUFF Thane of Fife
SIWARD an English general
MENTEITH a thane (nobleman of Scotland)
MACBETH
SOLDIERS in the armies of Malcolm and Macbeth

LANGUAGE

hew cut
wrack wreck, ruin
harness armour
clamorous harbingers noisy forerunners (trumpet blasts)
Lay on prepare to fight
usurper wrongful king (Macbeth)
Scone palace where Kings of Scotland were crowned (pronounced 'Scoon')

Pupils can use the military language to create an atmosphere of active conflict. The play ends with Malcolm's victory and rightful rule restored to Scotland.

TEACHING SUGGESTIONS

Whole class

The imaginative opportunities of this final scene are obvious: an army advancing under the camouflage of branches, a battle, victory celebrations and the coronation of Malcolm. Equally obvious is the need for teacher control to ensure that pupils' excitement does not result in chaos!

The most effective way of ensuring that the scene is staged safely, yet is full of action and thrilling dramatic effect, is to involve all pupils fully in discussion of the problems of staging. Ask them 'How can we act it in our classroom?'

Remind the class of what happens when actors rehearse and present battle scenes. Their supreme rule is 'safety first'. No-one must get hurt. So, only imaginary swords! Any fights can be rehearsed in slow motion.

Use pupil volunteers and lead a 'walk-through' of each of the four episodes. Incorporate suggestions from the class into the demonstration. Explain that on Shakespeare's stage, two or three actors represented an entire army.

- Birnam Wood: how does Malcolm's army enter? How do they carry out his instruction 'hew him down a bough'? Make the advance slow and ghost-like.

- Macbeth's defiance, the first battle: how does Macbeth react to the sight of Birnam Wood moving towards him? Your explanation of 'clamorous harbingers' can include that they are messengers who bring news that something is about to happen. Here it means the noise of trumpets, signalling that battle is about to begin.

- Macduff and Macbeth: Macbeth at first refuses to fight saying he has already killed too many of Macduff's family. But he rejects Macduff's demand to surrender ('yield').

- The victory and coronation: an opportunity for an impressive ceremony, beginning with the presentation of Macbeth's head (how?) and ending with Malcolm crowned.

Group work

Groups of six or more can act out the whole scene, or can take responsibility for one episode. Whatever organisation you adopt, ensure that 'battle' episodes are entirely safe. Some groups might incorporate the witches into the action.

Independent work

Use any worksheet from pages 96–107.

OR

Write a soldier's tale of the final battle.

The Tempest
Meet the characters

PROSPERO *(Duke of Milan)*
Graves at my command have waked their sleepers.

ARIEL *(an airy spirit, Prospero's servant)*
All hail, great master, grave sir, hail!

CALIBAN *(Prospero's slave)*
Knock a nail into his head!

MIRANDA *(Prospero's daughter)*
How beauteous mankind is! O brave new world!

ALONSO *(King of Naples)*
My son is lost, he's gone.

SEBASTIAN *(King Alonso's brother)*
Sir, you may thank yourself for this great loss.
The fault's your own.

ANTONIO *(Prospero's brother)*
I am right glad that he's so out of hope.

FERDINAND *(King Alonso's son)*
I am in my condition a prince, Miranda.

STEPHANO *(King Alonso's butler)*
Here's my comfort. (*drinks*)

TRINCULO *(King Alonso's jester)*
I have been in such a pickle since I saw you last.

GONZALO *(an old courtier)*
O rejoice beyond a common joy!

STORY

This introductory lesson on characters enables pupils to explore and hypothesise what the story of the play might be.

CHARACTERS

As named on the pupils' script.

LANGUAGE

condition social status

This lesson uses active methods to introduce major characters in the play. It helps pupils discover how Shakespeare creates character through language, and it enables them to speculate about what the characters are like, how they interact and how the story might develop.

TEACHING SUGGESTIONS

Whole class

Tell the class that they are going to get acquainted with some of the characters in *The Tempest* – and find out what they are like! Take each character in turn. Give pupils the name and brief description on the script, and speak their language. Pupils speak the line after you and strike a pose ('statue' or 'tableau') to portray the character who speaks. The portrayals can be done with pupils out of their seats, or sitting down if you prefer.

Don't be afraid to give pupils all kinds of prompts. What sort of person is Prospero who can bring alive dead people from their graves? Or Sebastian, who insists on telling his brother, who is grieving the loss of his son, that 'The fault's your own'?

Invite pupils to look at each others' 'statues' (this develops ideas about different ways of portrayal). Encourage class discussion of each character, asking pupils to give reasons for the sort of person they portray. Give the pupils plenty of practice, and use some of these active guessing 'games':

- Choose a character (without telling the class). Strike a pose, without speaking – pupils guess which character is portrayed, and the language spoken.

- Speak a line – pupils name the character.

- Describe a character, e.g. 'Duke of Milan' – pupils name the character.

- Name a character – pupils speak the character's line, and strike a pose.

- Choose two characters and set up a tableau to show them in relation to each other (for example, how might Prospero and Antonio behave together?).

- Invite pupils to create their own story – what sort of play has these characters in it?

Group work

Pairs or small groups work through their scripts, trying out poses and speaking the language. They play the 'guess the character' activities above.

Independent work

Use the language to make up your own story of what happens in the play.

OR

Choose one character. Write what you think happens to him or her in the play.

The Tempest
The play in ten actions!

Mercy on us! We split! we split! we split!

All hail, great master, grave sir, hail!

This island's mine!

Wherefore this ghastly looking?

Admired Miranda!

I'll kiss thy foot, thou wondrous man.

Knock a nail into his head!

I have made you mad.

I do forgive thee.

My Ariel, to the elements be free.

Our revels now are ended.

The Tempest The play in ten actions!

STORY

An opportunity for pupils to act out the whole play in ten actions!

CHARACTERS

As introduced in Teaching suggestions (right).

LANGUAGE

grave sir dignified master
ghastly looking
   frightful expressions
the elements
   sky and earth, fire and sea
revels entertainments

This is a lively and enjoyable introduction to the play. The vivid language from ten memorable moments in The Tempest *gives pupils active opportunities to play major characters and to acquire a sense of the structure of the play from beginning to end.*

Using frequent dramatic pauses, the teacher narrates the story (as in Teaching suggestions, right), and speaks the lines, adding actions and expressions to help pupils' own speaking and actions. Linking phrases like 'Meanwhile' or 'On another part of the island' help create atmosphere. After each line, all the pupils, in pairs, step into role, repeat the line, and act it out.

TEACHING SUGGESTIONS

Whole class

Add to the following teacher commentary as you wish:

1   Prospero is a great magician. His servant, Ariel, causes a terrible storm which wrecks the ship of King Alonso, Prospero's enemy. Everyone leaps overboard. 'Mercy on us! We split! we split! we split!' (Pupils speak and enact.)

2   Prospero is greeted by his servant Ariel, an airy spirit. 'All hail, great master, grave sir, hail!' (Pupils speak and enact master and servant.)

3   Prospero's slave, Caliban, thinks Prospero has stolen the island from him: 'This island's mine!' (Pupils speak and enact master and resentful slave.)

4   Meanwhile, King Alonso is asleep. His wicked brother Sebastian is about to kill him, when Alonso wakes up to find Sebastian with his sword drawn and looking very guilty. King Alonso asks 'Wherefore this ghastly looking?' (Pupils speak and pose as waking king and guilty brother.)

5   Prince Ferdinand the king's son has met and fallen in love with Prospero's daughter Miranda: 'Admired Miranda!' (Pupils speak and enact.)

6   Caliban has been made drunk by Stephano, the king's drunken butler. Caliban thinks Stephano is a god, and wants to worship him: 'I'll kiss thy foot, thou wondrous man.' (Pupils speak and enact.)

7   Caliban plots with Stephano to kill Prospero and become king of the island: 'Knock a nail into his head!' (Pupils rarely have difficulty enacting this!)

8   Ariel has driven Prospero's enemies into madness. He says to King Alonso: 'I have made you mad.' (Pupils show Ariel and demented Alonso.)

9   But Prospero is a kind man and although he has all his enemies in his power at the end of the play, he decides that forgiveness and mercy are much better than revenge. So he says to King Alonso: 'I do forgive thee.' (Pupils speak and enact forgiving Prospero and grateful Alonso.)

10 Even the drunken Stephano and Caliban are forgiven, and Prospero sets his faithful servant Ariel free to fly off and live happily: 'My Ariel, to the elements be free.' (Pupils speak and enact.)

And what do actors do at the end of a play? Yes! Take a bow and say:

'Our revels now are ended.' (Pupils make their own bow and farewell.)

Group work

In pairs or small groups, pupils rehearse and present 'the whole play'.

Independent work

Write the story of *The Tempest*. Include all the language you have learned.

The Tempest
Prospero versus Caliban

Thou poisonous slave!

A wicked dew drop on you!

Thou shalt be pinched!

A south-west blow on you!

Thou tortoise!

Blister you all over!

I'll rack thee with old cramps!

This island's mine!

Fill all thy bones with aches!

Toads, bats, beetles, light on you!

Make thee roar!

I know how to curse!

Hag-seed hence!

The red plague rid you!

The Tempest Prospero versus Caliban

STORY

This 'insults' activity leads to pupils telling their own stories about why the two characters hate each other so much.

CHARACTERS

PROSPERO Duke of Milan, exiled on a remote island

CALIBAN his slave who was born on the island before Prospero arrived

LANGUAGE

south-west biting wind
rack thee make you suffer
Hag-seed child of a witch
hence! clear off!

Students enjoy exchanging insults! The energetic power of Shakespeare's language, and the imaginative possibilities it provides, spark off pupils' own inventive and deductive powers as they make up their own insults and speculate about why these two people detest each other so much.

TEACHING SUGGESTIONS

Whole class

This can be a very noisy activity, so if you are unable to use the hall or drama studio, make sure your colleagues teaching in the next door classrooms are warned! If you do the lesson in the classroom and want the pupils to remain seated throughout, simply scale down and adapt the following activities.

First, speak as Prospero yourself, with the whole class speaking as Caliban. You will find your pupils eagerly seize the chance to insult their teacher!

Then divide the class into two halves. Each half lines up facing the other, with as much space as possible between the two lines (if pupils are seated in the classroom, define the line between the two groups). One group is Prospero, the other is Caliban. All the Prosperos speak their first insult 'Thou poisonous slave!' All the Calibans reply with 'A wicked dew drop on you!' The Prosperos call out 'Thou shalt be pinched!', and so on. Orchestrate a variety of ways for insults to be exchanged:

- Change roles – the Prosperos now become the Calibans.
- Pupils add gestures as they speak the language.
- The two groups turn back to back and call out insults without having eye contact.
- With each insult, each group steps one small pace towards the other group. The two lines will finish up in the middle of the room close together – so to avoid a breakdown of order, declare the rule: 'No touching!'
- Begin a class discussion. Which insult do you most enjoy speaking? Why? Why do these two people hate each other so much? Are there clues in the language?

Group work

Pupils work in pairs to practise different ways of delivering the insults: whispering them to each other, face to face; speaking them as if they were funny jokes; speaking them as sad stories; circling round each other speaking the insults. After these activities, pupils discuss what they think each character is like and why they hate each other so much.

Independent work

Pupils invent their own list of insults using Shakespeare's language as a model.

OR

Write your story of why Prospero and Caliban hate each other.

The Tempest
Ariel's story of the shipwreck

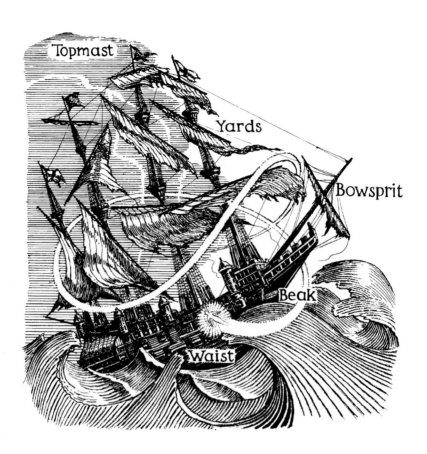

I boarded the king's ship. Now on the beak,
Now in the waist, the deck, in every cabin,
I flamed amazement. Sometime I'd divide
And burn in many places. On the topmast,
The yards and bowsprit, would I flame distinctly,
Then meet and join. Jove's lightnings, the precursors
Of the dreadful thunder-claps, more momentary
And sight-outrunning were not. The fire and cracks
Of sulphurous roaring the most mighty Neptune
Seem to besiege, and make his bold waves tremble,
Yea, his dread trident shake.
                       Not a soul
But felt a fever of the mad, and played
Some tricks of desperation. All but mariners
Plunged in the foaming brine and quit the vessel,
Then all a-fire with me. The king's son Ferdinand
With hair up-staring, was the first man that leaped,
Cried 'Hell is empty, and all the devils are here!'

The Tempest Ariel's story of the shipwreck

STORY

King Alonso's ship is sailing peacefully from Tunis to Naples. Ariel creates a tempest that overwhelms the vessel. All the passengers leap overboard in desperation to escape the burning ship.

CHARACTERS

ARIEL an airy spirit
PRINCE FERDINAND
   King Alonso's son
MARINERS
COURTIERS

LANGUAGE

beak, waist, topmast, yards, bowsprit see illustration
Jove King of the Gods (who throws thunderbolts)
precursors forerunners (lightning comes before thunder)
sulphurous roaring burning noise
Neptune King of the sea

Ariel's detailed description offers pupils thrilling opportunities to create their own staging of the shipwreck. Every one of the nine sentences is packed with action. The active verbs and imagination-stirring nouns invite performance.

TEACHING SUGGESTIONS

Whole class

Set the scene, adding as much imagined detail as you wish. King Alonso's court is sailing home to Naples after the marriage of the king's daughter Claribel to the King of Tunis. Ariel creates a terrible firestorm and sinks the ship.

To help pupils gain a first impression, speak the script a short section at a time, using actions and gestures. Ariel is probably breathless – he's just completed the huge task of creating a tempest! Pupils repeat your words and actions.

There is an all-too-obvious problem with this scene, so share it with the class: 'How can we stage the shipwreck in our classroom?' Incorporate pupils' suggestions into a teacher-led demonstration. Use pupil volunteers (two as Ariel, two sailors, two courtiers and Ferdinand) to act out the language in a small space at the front or in the middle of the room. Some hints:

- Create an imaginary ship. The crew works, the courtiers relax.
- 'I boarded the King's ship.' – the Ariels step delicately on board.
- 'Now on the beak … in every cabin,' – Ariels move from place to place.
- 'I flamed amazement.' – Ariels use hands, arms, faces to show 'flamed'. The crew and courtiers are amazed at what they see.
- 'Sometime I'd divide … many places.' – the two Ariels separate and show 'fire'.
- 'On the topmast … meet and join.' – the Ariels reach up (topmast), stretch out (yards) and point forward (bowsprit). They 'flame' (hand movements), then link hands.
- 'Jove's lightnings', 'dreadful thunder-claps' and 'fire and cracks Of sulphurous roaring' can be hand movements and sound effects by the whole class.
- 'more momentary And sight-outrunning' – a huge challenge! How can pupils mime the speed of light that is too fast for the eye to catch?
- Bring in a pupil to portray 'The most mighty Neptune' shaking his 'dread trident'. Direct the final seven lines in short sections to show everyone going mad and the courtiers and Ferdinand leaping overboard.

Group work

Groups of six to ten pupils work out their own performances of Ariel's story.

Individual work

Use any worksheet from pages 96–107.

OR

Write a sailor's story of his experience of the shipwreck.

The Tempest
Prospero is overthrown

Twelve year since, Miranda, twelve year since,
Thy father was the Duke of Milan, and
A prince of power.

I, neglecting worldly ends, all dedicated
To closeness, and the bettering of my mind,
Being transported and rapt in secret studies,
The government I cast upon my brother.
My brother, and thy uncle, called Antonio –
That a brother should be so perfidious!

In my false brother awaked an evil nature.
He did believe he was indeed the Duke.
Hence his ambition growing, he needs will be
Absolute Milan. He thinks me now incapable,
Confederates with the King of Naples
– an enemy to me inveterate –
That he should presently extirpate me and mine
Out of the dukedom, and confer fair Milan,
With all the honours, on my brother.

Whereon, a treacherous army levied,
One midnight fated to the purpose,
Did Antonio open the gates of Milan,
And in the dead of darkness hurried thence
Me and thy crying self.

They hurried us aboard a barque,
Bore us some leagues to sea, where they prepared
A rotten carcass of a butt, not rigged,
Nor tackle, sail, nor mast – the very rats
Instinctively have quit it. Some food we had,
And some fresh water, that a noble Neapolitan,
Gonzalo, out of his charity did give us.
Here in this island we arrived, and here
Bountiful Fortune hath mine enemies
Brought to this shore.

The Tempest Prospero is overthrown

STORY

Prospero tells Miranda that he neglected his duties as Duke of Milan because he was so interested in studying. His wicked brother Antonio joined with the King of Naples to overthrow him. Aided by the kind old Gonzalo, and after a perilous sea journey, Prospero and Miranda landed on the island. Now his enemies are in his power.

CHARACTERS

PROSPERO Duke of Milan
MIRANDA his daughter
ANTONIO his wicked brother
ALONSO King of Naples
GONZALO a good old courtier
SOLDIERS, COURTIERS, RATS

LANGUAGE

neglecting worldly ends
   not doing my duties as Duke
closeness privacy
transported and rapt in
   enchanted and wrapped up in
perfidious treacherous
Absolute Milan
   the only ruler of Milan
Confederates joins
inveterate by long custom
extirpate expel
levied recruited
barque small ship
leagues sea-miles
carcass of a butt shell of a boat
not rigged, Nor tackle
   without equipment

As they act out how Antonio seized Milan and exiled Prospero, pupils extend their vocabulary in active and enjoyable ways: 'transported and rapt', 'perfidious', 'confederates with', 'inveterate', etc.

TEACHING SUGGESTIONS

Whole class

The script is set out to help pupils understand and enact the five different 'events': the mighty Duke, the neglectful ruler, the conspiracy, the overthrow, the sea journey. Speak the language in small sections, calling on volunteer pupils to step into role as required, and using ideas contributed by the class. Some hints:

- 'A prince of power.' – two or three pupils bow, salute, cry 'Long live Prospero'.
- 'I neglecting … studies,' – pupil shows Prospero utterly absorbed in his books.
- 'The government … perfidious!' – demonstrate a 'perfidious' look; pupils imitate.
- 'He did believe … Milan.' – Antonio swells with pride, bosses courtiers around.
- 'He thinks … Naples' – pupils whisper slyly ('confederates' can also mean 'makes secret plan').
- 'an enemy … inveterate' – Alonso threatens Prospero ('inveterate' can mean confirmed, or age-long, or traditional, or habitual).
- 'That he should … brother.' – Alonso and Antonio mime expelling Prospero from Milan. Alonso crowns Antonio. The courtiers salute him.
- 'Whereon … levied,' – Antonio and Alonso gather an army (two pupils!).
- 'One midnight … Milan,' – Antonio mimes opening gates, the soldiers march in.
- 'And in … self.' – soldiers capture Prospero and Miranda and march them out.
- 'They … barque … sea,' – all step into imaginary boat and row away.
- 'where they … rats … it.' – two pupils, as rats, jump overboard, squealing, and swim away. Miranda and Prospero are placed on board. Soldiers row off.
- 'Some food … us.' – Gonzalo rows out, hands over food and water.
- 'Here on this island we arrived,' – mime sea journey and arrival on shore.
- 'and here … shore.' – Antonio and Alonso stagger in, fall at Prospero's feet.

Group work

Divide the class into four groups, each with responsibility to enact a part of the story set out in the pupils' script (one group has the first nine lines).

Individual work

Use any worksheet from pages 96–107.

OR

Write the treaty in which Alonso and Antonio agree to overthrow Prospero.

The Tempest
What did Sycorax do?

This foul witch Sycorax, who with age and envy
Was grown into a hoop, for mischiefs manifold,
And sorceries terrible to enter human hearing,
From Algiers, thou knowest, was banished.
For one thing she did, they would not take her life.

The Tempest What did Sycorax do?

STORY

In Algiers, Sycorax plays all kinds of tricks and practises terrifying witchcraft. The citizens want to kill her, but because of one thing she did, they spare her life and only banish her from the city.

CHARACTERS

SYCORAX a witch (who might
    have spirits to help her)
CITIZENS of Algiers

LANGUAGE

mischiefs manifold
    many mischiefs (wicked tricks)
banished
    exiled from the city and
    ordered never to return (see
    page 4)

The simple language of the final line evokes wonderfully imaginative responses from the pupils. You will find their presentations are often variations on 'bringing the king's dead child back to life', or 'slaying a monster that threatens the city', or 'calming the storm'. But every one will be fresh and new to the pupils – it is their own!

TEACHING SUGGESTIONS

Whole class

Tell the class they are going to solve a mystery that has puzzled people for nearly 400 years: what was the 'one thing' done by a terrifying witch that saved her life when she was under sentence of death?

Speak the five lines to the class. Speak them again, a short section at a time with the pupils repeating your words and any actions. Put as much feeling as you can into each imagination-provoking word: 'foul', 'envy', 'mischiefs manifold', etc. Then invite the pupils to respond to each section. Encourage them to let their imaginations run, so that they build up an impression of the terrifying witch who was so feared in Algiers:

- Her name – ask them to roll 'Sycorax' round their tongues. What does it sound like? Does it give a clue to what she's like?
- 'with ... envy' – why should envy make her like a hoop? Ask pupils to give practical examples of envy.
- 'mischiefs manifold' – what were the many tricks and crimes she did: not just a few, but many ('manifold')?
- 'sorceries terrible to enter human hearing' – what were Sycorax' sorceries: the spells and magic that filled the people of Algiers with terror?

Fire pupils' imaginations with the final two lines. The citizens were utterly enraged with all Sycorax' 'mischiefs' and 'sorceries'. They wanted to kill her, but they spared her life and only banished her because:

  'For one thing she did, they would not take her life.'

What was that 'one thing' she did? Invite suggestions from the whole class. These suggestions will provide a rich resource for group work.

Group work

Groups of six to ten pupils work out their portrayals of Sycorax. Encourage them to use a narrator to speak the five lines. The narrator pauses after 'mischiefs manifold' and 'sorceries' and the group shows one or two examples of each. Pupils then act out their version of the 'one thing she did' that made the citizens decide to spare her life. The results can be electrifying!

Individual work

Use any worksheet from pages 96–107.

OR

Write the public proclamation that tells of Sycorax' crimes, her banishment, and why she is spared execution.

The Tempest
Sycorax imprisons Ariel

This blue-eyed hag was hither brought with child,
And here was left by the sailors. Thou my slave,
As thou reportest thyself, was then her servant.
And for thou wast a spirit too delicate
To act her earthy and abhorred commands,
Refusing her grand hests, she did confine thee,
By help of her more potent ministers,
And in her most unmitigable rage,
Into a cloven pine.

         Within which rift
Imprisoned thou didst painfully remain
A dozen years. Within which space she died,
And left thee there, where thou didst vent thy groans
As fast as mill-wheels strike.

Thou best knowest what torment I did find thee in.
Thy groans did make wolves howl,
And penetrate the breasts of ever-angry bears.
It was a torment to lay upon the damned.
It was mine art, when I arrived and heard thee,
That made gape the pine, and let thee out.

The Tempest Sycorax imprisons Ariel

STORY

Prospero tells how the witch Sycorax came to the island, and made Ariel her slave. When Ariel refused to obey her, she imprisoned him in a split pine tree where he suffered in agony. Sycorax died, but Prospero, using his magic, released Ariel from captivity.

CHARACTERS

SYCORAX a witch
ARIEL an airy spirit
SPIRITS servants of Sycorax
    ('potent ministers')
PROSPERO Duke of Milan and a
    great magician

LANGUAGE

earthy and abhorred commands
    unpleasant and hateful orders
grand hests horrible orders
unmitigable unquenchable
cloven pine split tree
vent thy groans
    cry out your agony
art magic power

*The scene is full of striking
phrases that spur pupils'
imaginations: 'earthy and
abhorred commands', 'most
unmitigable rage', 'cloven pine',
'as fast as mill-wheels strike',
'ever-angry bears', etc.*

TEACHING SUGGESTIONS

Whole class

Work through the story a sentence at a time (remind the class that it is Prospero who is telling the story). Use pupil volunteers to act out each sentence, incorporating suggestions from the class.

- First sentence: pupils show Sycorax and her son Caliban being ferried over the sea by sailors and abandoned on the island.

- Second sentence: a pupil, as Ariel, acts as Sycorax' servant.

- Third sentence: the 'delicate' Ariel is given all kinds of unpleasant and hateful tasks ('earthy and abhorred commands'), but finally refuses to carry out Sycorax' most horrible orders. So Sycorax imprisons Ariel, helped by her powerful spirit attendants ('potent ministers'). She is in a towering rage. Get everyone in the class to show what 'a rage' looks like – then ask them to show an 'unmitigable rage' – then a 'most unmitigable rage'! Make sure you don't let control slip; 30 young pupils all showing an 'unmitigable rage' can be an awesome experience! Two pupils can act as the 'cloven pine': Sycorax splits the 'tree', and pins Ariel inside it.

- Fourth and fifth sentence: Ariel suffers and Sycorax dies. Can pupils mime mill-wheels striking as Ariel groans?

- Final four sentences: Prospero arrives on the island and finds Ariel in agony (pupils play wolves howling and fierce bears showing pity). Prospero uses his magic ('mine art') to release Ariel.

Group work

Each small group works out their presentation of the lines. Two pupils might act as narrators while the others perform the actions.

Independent work

Use any worksheet from pages 96–107.

OR

Step into role as Ariel and write the story of what happened to you.

The Tempest
This island's mine!

As wicked dew as e'er my mother brushed
With raven's feather from unwholesome fen,
Drop on you both! A south-west blow on ye,
And blister you all over!

This island's mine by Sycorax my mother,
Which thou took from me. When thou came first,
Thou stroked me, and made much of me.
Would give me water with berries in it,
And teach me how to name the bigger light,
And how the less, that burn by day and night.

And then I loved thee,
And showed thee all the qualities of the isle,
The fresh springs, brine-pits, barren place and fertile.
Cursed be I that did so!

                    All the charms
Of Sycorax – toads, beetles, bats – light on you!
For I am all the subjects that you have,
Which first was mine own king.
And here you sty me in this hard rock,
Whiles you do keep from me the rest of the isle.

You taught me language, and my profit of it
Is, I know how to curse. The red plague rid you
For learning me your language!

The Tempest This island's mine!

STORY

Caliban rages at Prospero and Miranda, saying they stole the island from him. He tells how they were kind to him when they first arrived, and he showed them all over the island. But Prospero made him a slave.

CHARACTERS

CALIBAN who was born on the island

PROSPERO Duke of Milan

MIRANDA his daughter

LANGUAGE

unwholesome fen
  unhealthy marsh
south-west very strong hot wind
the bigger light the sun
the less the moon
qualities fine features
sty me keep me like a pig

Caliban's inventive curses help pupils experience his anger and rage. But his language also expresses the tenderness and kindness of his first meetings with Prospero.

TEACHING SUGGESTIONS

Whole class

The pupils' script is set out in five sections or paragraphs, each of which can be spoken and acted by pupils to create a different mood. The teacher first speaks each section in short units, with the whole class repeating words and actions. Pupils then contribute ideas on how each section might be staged. Some hints:

- Paragraph 1: divide the first sentence into very short units, each accompanied with an action (e.g. flutter your fingers for 'As wicked dew', and hold your nose for 'from unwholesome fen'). After all the pupils have repeated your words and gestures, one half of the class, speaking in unison, can rage at the other half. Alternatively pupils can work in pairs to 'curse' each other.

- Paragraph 2: as you speak each short section, bring out the emotional tone of each, e.g. anger ('This island's mine'), tenderness ('by Sycorax my mother'), resentment ('Which thou took from me'). Use volunteer pupils to mime Sycorax, just before she dies, handing over the island to her son. Caliban weeps for her, but gains comfort from looking over his island. Prospero comes ashore with Miranda. They are kind to Caliban, give him drink and teach him language (e.g. naming the sun and moon).

- Paragraph 3: Caliban is affectionate towards Prospero and Miranda and shows them all kinds of places on the isle: 'fresh springs', 'brine-pits', 'barren place' and 'fertile' (invent different reactions to each place). Is Prospero seen making up his mind to take over the island?

- Paragraph 4: Caliban rages at Prospero, who has enslaved him, imprisoning him in a 'hard rock' and preventing his attempts to escape. Again, speak very short units, with gestures, for pupils to repeat. Your actions will make clear the meanings of such phrases as 'light on you' (land on you) without need for verbal explanation.

- Paragraph 5: more angry cursing. Use the punctuation as a guide to speaking short units. Speak the last sentence as a whole. This is another opportunity for pairs or groups to insult each other (as in paragraph 1).

Group work

Groups of three or more pupils rehearse and present their version of the script. Ask them to show in their performances whether they think that Caliban has been fairly treated.

Independent work

Use any worksheet from pages 96–107.

OR

Who really owns the island? Write Caliban's story of what happened.

The Tempest
Falling in love

ARIEL	Full fathom five thy father lies,
	Of his bones are coral made.
	Those are pearls that were his eyes,
	Nothing of him that doth fade,
	But doth suffer a sea-change
	Into something rich and strange.
	Sea-nymphs hourly ring his knell
	Hark, now I hear them, 'ding dong bell'.
FERDINAND	Where should this music be?
	In the air or the earth? (*He sees Miranda*)
	Most sure, the goddess on whom these airs attend.
	Oh you wonder!
MIRANDA	No wonder sir, but certainly a maid.
FERDINAND	My language? Heavens!
	I'll make you the Queen of Naples.
PROSPERO	Thou hast put thyself upon this island
	As a spy, to win it from me, the lord of it.
	I'll manacle thy neck and feet together.
	Sea water shalt thou drink. Thy food shall be
	The fresh-brook mussels, withered roots, and husks.
	(*Ferdinand is made to carry logs. Prospero watches, unseen.*)
MIRANDA	Work not so hard. I'll bear your logs.
	My father's of a better nature, sir, than he appears.
FERDINAND	What is your name?
MIRANDA	Miranda.
FERDINAND	Admired Miranda. I am in my condition
	A prince, Miranda. The very instant that I saw you
	Did my heart fly to your service.
MIRANDA	Do you love me?
FERDINAND	Beyond all limit of what else in the world,
	I do love, prize, honour you.
MIRANDA	I am your wife, if you will marry me.
FERDINAND	Here's my hand.
MIRANDA	And mine, with my heart in it.
PROSPERO	All thy vexations were but my trials of thy love.
	Take my daughter. She is thine own.

The Tempest Falling in love

STORY

Ariel sings of Ferdinand's drowned father. Ferdinand falls in love at first sight with Miranda, but Prospero punishes him. Miranda offers to help Ferdinand, and they agree to marry. Prospero reveals that the punishment was only a test of Ferdinand's love.

CHARACTERS

FERDINAND son of King Alonso
MIRANDA daughter of Prospero
PROSPERO Duke of Milan
ARIEL an airy spirit

LANGUAGE

knell bell tolling (ringing)
at a funeral
these airs attend
this music serves
manacle chain with iron hoops
vexations troubles, hardships
trials tests

Ariel's song is very rhythmical. It can make a lesson on its own. Small groups speak or sing the lines, repeating phrases, making up their own tunes, and accompanying with sound effects (waves, wind whistling, bells, humming, etc.). The love scene is a 'quiet', sincere activity, making challenging demands on pupils' emotions.

TEACHING SUGGESTIONS

Whole class

Speak Ariel's song line by line as rhythmically as you can. The whole class repeats each line and rhythm. Spend some time exploring different ways in which everyone in the class can join in a choral speaking presentation of the song (see page 8).

The dialogue involves only three speaking characters. Choose two pupil volunteers to play Ferdinand and Miranda, and act as Prospero and director yourself. Provide a running commentary to guide the actors, and enable all the class to understand what happens.

Ferdinand is very sad. He thinks his father has been drowned, and the words of Ariel's song makes him grieve even more. He is struck with wonder when he sees Miranda, and amazed that she can speak his language (ask pupils 'why?').

Make Prospero's accusation and punishment of Ferdinand a harsh episode. Ferdinand can carry anything available in the classroom, e.g. a pile of books.

The sequence between Miranda and Ferdinand needs delicate handling. Make it as sincere as possible. Avoid 'sending it up' even though it can present difficulties for younger pupils. Tell them that Shakespeare creates all kinds of moods in his plays, and here he wants the meeting to be as tender and sincere as possible. Encourage your actors to pause as long as they can before they speak. For example, Miranda could pause for some time before she tells her name because her father forbade her to have anything to do with Ferdinand.

End the episode with Prospero blessing the engagement of the couple. Speak the lines in a dignified way and add actions, for example taking the hands of Ferdinand and Miranda to join them in marriage. Ariel might join the group so that the final moment is a tableau of the 'engagement' – a happy moment!

Group work

Groups of four or more explore ways of speaking or singing Ariel's song. They then work out how to present their version of the meeting of Ferdinand and Miranda.

Independent work

Use any worksheet from pages 96–107.

OR

Write a ballad that tells how Ferdinand and Miranda met and fell in love.

The Tempest
Ariel accuses Prospero's enemies

Solemn and strange music. Enter several strange shapes, bringing in a banquet. They dance about it with gentle actions of salutations, inviting the king and others to eat. They depart.

ALONSO Give us kind keepers, heavens! What were these?

SEBASTIAN A living drollery! Now I will believe that there are unicorns.

ALONSO Such shapes, such gesture, and such sound.

ANTONIO Will it please you taste of what is here?

ALONSO I will stand to, and feed.

Thunder and lightning Enter ARIEL like a harpy, claps his wings upon the table, and with a quaint device the banquet vanishes.

ARIEL You are three men of sin, unfit to live,
And on this island, where man doth not inhabit,
I have made you mad.

Alonso, Sebastian and Antonio draw their swords.

You fools! I and my fellows are ministers of fate.
Your swords may as well wound the loud winds,
As diminish one dowl that's in my plume.
Your swords are now too massy for your strengths
And will not be uplifted. But remember –
You three from Milan did supplant good Prospero.
Exposed unto the sea him and his innocent child.
For which foul deed, the powers, delaying, not forgetting,
Have incensed the seas and shores, yea, all the creatures
Against your peace. Thee of thy son, Alonso,
They have bereft, and do pronounce by me
Lingering perdition, unless you show
Heart's sorrow, and a clear life ensuing.

Ariel vanishes in thunder; then to soft music, enter the shapes again, and dance, with mocks and mows, and then depart carrying out the table. Alonso and the others leave in great desperation.

The Tempest Ariel accuses Prospero's enemies

STORY

Ariel and his spirits conjure up a magical banquet. Just as King Alonso prepares to eat, the banquet vanishes and Ariel accuses him and Sebastian and Antonio of their crimes against Prospero. He condemns them to long-lasting suffering unless they repent.

CHARACTERS

KING ALONSO
SEBASTIAN } enemies of
ANTONIO   } Prospero
ARIEL an airy spirit
SPIRITS who appear as strange
shapes

LANGUAGE

kind keepers gentle guards
drollery puppet show
harpy a monster with a woman's
face, wings and claws of a
vulture
dowl tiny feather
plume headdress
supplant overthrow
incensed made angry
bereft stolen
Lingering perdition slow ruin
clear life ensuing
good life from now on
mocks and mows
pulling funny faces

Ariel speaks like a judge delivering a harsh sentence. His tone is commanding and accusatory. He condemns the three men for seizing Prospero's dukedom and exposing him and his daughter Miranda to the dangers of the sea.

TEACHING SUGGESTIONS

Whole class

Remind the class of story so far (Prospero was overthrown by the three men who are now shipwrecked on the island and in Prospero's power. Will he seek revenge?). Then consider in turn the five episodes, asking your pupils for ideas on how each could be staged and spoken.

- Opening stage direction: what do the 'strange shapes' look like? How do they move and dance? What kind of banquet do they bring in? How might it be staged in the classroom?

- The amazement of Prospero's enemies: speak the lines several times in short sections with the pupils repeating your words. Ask individual volunteers to speak in as incredulous a tone as possible. Can the pupils guess why Sebastian is now ready to believe in unicorns?

- Second stage direction: remind pupils what a harpy looks like (see left, but there are other possibilities). Ask how they could stage the banquet vanishing ('quaint device' = strange trick).

- Ariel's speech: speak it a short section at a time, with the class repeating after you. Several volunteers might act what each section describes. This can include the three men forcing Prospero and his daughter out of Milan; their perilous sea-journey; the gods ('the powers') making the sea angry and shipwrecking the three men on the island, and drowning Alonso's son, Ferdinand (he is not really drowned, but Alonso thinks so).

- The final stage direction: how does Ariel vanish? How do the shapes dance, and what faces do they pull? (You will have no shortage of volunteers to show you 'mocks and mows'!) How do the 'three men of sin' leave the stage?

Group work

Groups of six or more enjoy working on the practical problems of this scene: how to stage the spectacle called for by the stage directions. Alternatively, you can have groups working on Ariel's accusation and judgement. Several pupils share Ariel's lines, three pupils are the enemies of Prospero: how do they react? Are they likely to repent?

Independent work

Use any worksheet from pages 96–107.

OR

Imagine you are King Alonso. Tell your story of the scene.

The Tempest
The wedding masque

Ferdinand and Miranda watch as PROSPERO *calls in the actors in the masque.*

PROSPERO	No tongue! All eyes! Be silent!
IRIS	The queen of the sky,
	Whose watery arch and messenger am I,
	Bids thee here on this grass-plot
	To come and sport. Her peacocks fly amain.
	Approach, rich Ceres, her to entertain.
CERES	Hail, many-coloured messenger. Why hath thy queen
	Summoned me hither, to this short-grazed green?
IRIS	A contract of true love to celebrate.
	Highest queen of state, great Juno comes.

JUNO descends.

JUNO	Honour, riches, marriage-blessing,
	Long continuance and increasing,
	Hourly joys be still upon you,
	Juno sings her blessings on you
CERES	Earth's increase, and foison plenty,
	Barns and garners never empty.
	Spring come to you at the farthest,
	In the very end of harvest.
	Scarcity and want shall shun you
	Ceres' blessing so is on you
IRIS	Come, temperate nymphs, and help to celebrate
	A contract of true love. Be not too late.

Enter nymphs.

You sun-burned sicklemen of August weary,
Come hither from the furrow, and be merry.

Enter reapers. They join with the nymphs in a graceful dance to celebrate the marriage.

The Tempest The wedding masque

STORY

Prospero arranges a masque to celebrate the forthcoming wedding of Ferdinand and Miranda. Three goddesses bless and honour the couple, and the ceremony ends with a dance of nymphs and harvestmen.

CHARACTERS

PROSPERO Duke of Milan
MIRANDA his daughter
FERDINAND a prince
IRIS goddess of the rainbow
CERES goddess of harvest
JUNO goddess of the sky
NYMPHS female spirits
REAPERS harvestmen

LANGUAGE

watery arch rainbow
amain speedily
short-grazed
   closely nibbled grass
foison abundant harvest
garners grain stores
shun avoid
temperate nymphs cool spirits
sicklemen harvestmen

The formal, ceremonious language is appropriate to the speakers (goddesses) and to the occasion (a dignified celebration of a forthcoming royal marriage). Pupils can explore how to combine appropriate movement and dance with their speaking of the lines.

TEACHING SUGGESTIONS

Whole class

The masque provides an opportunity for the whole class to work together to pre-pare a presentation that can be shown to other classes, to parents or at a festival.

Tell the class about masques in Shakespeare's day. Masques were spectacular celebrations involving speaking, singing, dancing, and fantastic costumes. Prospero's masque enables pupils to enter into the spirit, language and style of the spectacles that were presented at the court of King James I.

Help the pupils gain a first impression by speaking the lines with the whole class repeating each short section after you. Then set the practical question of how the whole class can be involved in a performance. Invite and incorporate pupils' suggestions. For example, they might suggest beginning with a narrator setting the scene:

> 'Prospero, the exiled Duke of Milan, and a great magician, arranges a masque to celebrate the wedding of his daughter Miranda to Prince Ferdinand.'

Prospero enters, leading in Ferdinand and Miranda. He calls in all the actors, and says to Ferdinand and Miranda:

> 'No tongue! All eyes! Be silent!'

Prospero repeats that order to the audience (the six words often become a shared class joke as the teacher uses them in other lessons) – and the masque begins. How do Iris and Ceres enter, how are they dressed (clues in 'rainbow' and 'harvest')? How might Juno 'descend'?

Group work

Divide the class into five roughly equal groups. Give each group a role: Iris, Ceres, Juno, Nymphs, Reapers. Each group works out how it will speak and act. One pupil who plays Prospero can be adviser to the groups.

The goddesses repeat lines, sing and move to create a celestial show. The nymphs and shepherds work out a dance, but also invent language to speak or sing. For example, they might repeat Juno's blessing, substituting 'We all' for 'Juno' and 'our' for 'her'. The masque should end with a striking tableau in which everyone is involved.

Independent work

Use any worksheet from pages 96–107.

OR

Write six to ten lines of your own for another goddess or god to speak.

The Tempest
Prospero defeats Caliban

ARIEL *hangs glistering apparel on a line. The plotters enter.*

CALIBAN   I am subject to a tyrant, a sorcerer, that by his cunning hath cheated me of the island. Thou shalt be lord of it, and I'll serve thee. Knock a nail into his head.

STEPHANO   Monster, I will kill this man. His daughter and I will be king and queen, and Trinculo and thyself shall be viceroys.

CALIBAN   Pray you tread softly, that the blind mole may not hear a foot fall. Speak softly. All's hushed as midnight yet.

TRINCULO   O King Stephano! Look what a wardrobe here is for thee.

CALIBAN   Let it alone, thou fool, it is but trash.

STEPHANO   Put off that gown, Trinculo! By this hand I'll have that gown.

CALIBAN   Let it alone, and do the murder first!

STEPHANO   Be you quiet, monster.

CALIBAN   We shall lose our time, and all be turned to barnacles.

Stephano and Trinculo enjoy trying on the clothes.
A noise of hunters heard. Enter diverse spirits in the shape of dogs and hounds. They chase Caliban, Stephano and Trinculo around the stage. Prospero and Ariel urge them on.

PROSPERO   Hey, Mountain, hey!

ARIEL   Silver! There it goes, Silver!

PROSPERO   Fury, Fury! There, Tyrant, there! Hark, hark!
Let them be hunted soundly. At this hour
Lies at my mercy all my enemies.
Shortly shall all my labours end, and thou,
My Ariel, shall have the air at freedom.

Stepping into Shakespeare © Cambridge University Press 2000. See notice on p. ii

The Tempest Prospero defeats Caliban

STORY

Caliban has persuaded Stephano to kill Prospero and become king of the island. But Ariel hangs glittering costumes on a line, and Stephano and Trinculo eagerly try on the clothes, forgetting their murderous plan. Prospero and Ariel encourage spirits, disguised as hunting dogs, to drive away the plotters.

CHARACTERS

CALIBAN Prospero's slave
STEPHANO a drunken butler
TRINCULO a jester
PROSPERO Duke of Milan
ARIEL his servant, an airy spirit
SPIRITS disguised as hunting
    dogs (Mountain, Silver, Fury,
    Tyrant)

LANGUAGE

glistering apparel
    colourful clothes
subject slave
sorcerer magician
viceroys deputy kings
barnacles barnacle geese
diverse various
soundly thoroughly

The scene is fun to act. Caliban's remarkable image 'Tread softly, that the blind mole may not hear a foot fall' can stir pupils' imagination in their performance and in their writing.

TEACHING SUGGESTIONS

Whole class

Set the scene, reminding the pupils that the three plotters intend to kill Prospero and take over the island. Use pupil volunteers to act out suggestions from the class as you work through the scene:

- 'Ariel hangs glistering apparel on a line.' – there's much fun to be had from two or more pupils presenting themselves as a line of washing!

- 'The plotters enter.' – remind the class that it has to be a dramatic entry. Ask pupils 'What do these three people intend to do? How will that affect the way they enter?'

Speak the language a short section at a time with pupils repeating your tone and gestures. Show by your delivery that the language is the clue to what the characters are like. For example, Caliban's first three sentences can have very different tones: aggrieved, flattering and angry.

Direct pupil volunteers how to perform their plotting, and how Stephano and Trinculo are distracted by the sight of the colourful clothes (plenty of opportunities for comedy as they try on the clothes).

- Staging the hunt: have the pupil volunteers perform the chase in slow motion to avoid the chaos that can result from over-exuberance! Ask for suggestions how each 'spirit/dog' might enter and move to match its name (Mountain, Silver, Fury, Tyrant). How does each plotter try to escape?

- Prospero's final four lines: what does he intend to do with all his enemies now they are at his mercy? The answer will be revealed in the next lesson. How does Ariel react to being promised his freedom?

Group work

Pupils work in groups of six or more to prepare their versions of the scene. Another reminder: it is sensible to insist on a slow motion chase.

Independent work

Use any worksheet from pages 96–107.

OR

Write a story of how a murder is prevented by a clever trick.

OR

Write a story that includes each of the following words: 'sorcerer', 'viceroy', 'mole', 'wardrobe', 'barnacles', 'hunted', 'mercy', 'freedom'.

The Tempest
Prospero forgives his enemies

Solemn music. PROSPERO *uses his staff to trace out a large circle.*

PROSPERO   This rough magic I here abjure.
I'll break my staff, and deeper than
Did ever plummet sound, I'll drown my book.

Enter ARIEL, *then* ALONSO *with a frantic gesture, and*
SEBASTIAN *and* ANTONIO. *They all enter the circle and there*
stand charmed. Ariel leaves.

PROSPERO   There stand, for you are spell-stopped.
Behold, sir king, the wrongèd Duke of Milan, Prospero.
Most cruelly didst thou, Alonso, use me and my daughter.
Flesh and blood, you, brother mine,
Who with Sebastian would here have killed your king,
I do forgive thee. Welcome my friends all.

Prospero reveals FERDINAND *and* MIRANDA *playing at chess.*

MIRANDA   O wonder!
How many goodly creatures are there here!
How beauteous mankind is! O brave new world
That has such people in it.

Enter ARIEL *driving in* CALIBAN, STEPHANO *and* TRINCULO.

PROSPERO   Two of these fellows you must know and own.
This thing of darkness, I acknowledge mine.

TRINCULO   I have been in such a pickle since I saw you last.

STEPHANO   O touch me not! I am not Stephano, but a cramp.

PROSPERO   (*To Caliban*) Go sirrah to my cell. As you look
To have my pardon, trim it handsomely.

CALIBAN   Ay, that I will, and I'll be wise hereafter,
And seek for grace.

PROSPERO   Sir, I invite your highness and your train
To my poor cell. And in the morn
I'll bring you to your ship, and so to Naples
To see the nuptial of these our dear beloved.
My Ariel, to the elements be free, and fare you well.

STORY

Prospero gives up his magic powers. Ariel brings Alonso, Antonio and Sebastian (Prospero's enemies) into a magic circle drawn by Prospero, who forgives and welcomes them. He reveals the newly-engaged Ferdinand and Miranda. Ariel drives in the three comic plotters, and Prospero forgives them. He releases Ariel to freedom.

CHARACTERS

PROSPERO Duke of Milan
ARIEL his servant
MIRANDA his daughter
FERDINAND son of King Alonso

Enemies of Prospero who overthrew and exiled him
ALONSO King of Naples
SEBASTIAN his brother
ANTONIO Prospero's brother

Plotters against Prospero's life
CALIBAN Prospero's slave
STEPHANO a drunken butler
TRINCULO a jester

LANGUAGE

abjure give up
plummet line used to measure ('sound') depth of the sea
spell-stopped magically frozen
trim it handsomely
    tidy and clean it well
train attendants
cell cave
nuptial wedding

The mood of this final scene is one of welcome, forgiveness and reconciliation.

TEACHING SUGGESTIONS

Whole class

Take a 'directing' role, and use pupils' suggestions to help volunteers 'walk through' the scene so that the class can understand its five episodes. Speak the language in short sections, with actions, for all the class to repeat.

- Prospero's renunciation of his magic powers: ask pupils to invent a ceremony for how Prospero 'traces out a circle', and what he does with his magic staff and his book of secret magic.

- The entry and forgiving of Alonso, Sebastian and Antonio: how might the three disturbed noblemen enter and 'stand charmed'? What gestures accompany 'Behold' as Prospero reveals his identity? He speaks first to Alonso, then to his brother Antonio ('Flesh and blood'), who, with Sebastian had earlier plotted to kill Alonso. What actions might he use as he forgives and welcomes the three men?

- The revealing of Ferdinand and Miranda: how, in the classroom, might this be done? Remind the pupils that Miranda is talking about men who overthrew Prospero and plotted murder. How do they (and Prospero) react to her words ('goodly creatures' and 'brave new world')?

- The entry and forgiving of Caliban, Stephano and Trinculo: should this episode be funny or serious? Ask pupils to use the clues in the language to suggest their answer.

- Prospero's promise of happiness ahead and his setting free of Ariel: he speaks first to King Alonso (the master of Stephano and Trinculo), then to Ariel. How does Ariel react to being given his freedom, and how does everyone leave the stage?

Group work

Groups of ten or more pupils work out their stagings of the scene. Alternatively, pupils can work in pairs or small groups and make a list of all the 'rough magic' that Prospero gives up (the contents of his 'book' of secrets).

Independent work

Use any worksheet from pages 96–107.

OR

Step into role as Prospero and write your secret diary entry telling your reasons for forgiving, rather than punishing your enemies.

The Tempest
Farewell to the audience

Our revels now are ended. These our actors,
As I foretold you, were all spirits, and
Are melted into air, into thin air;
And like the baseless fabric of this vision,
The cloud-capped towers, the gorgeous palaces,
The solemn temples, the great globe itself,
Yea, all which it inherit, shall dissolve,
And like this insubstantial pageant faded
Leave not a rack behind. We are such stuff
As dreams are made on, and our little life
Is rounded with a sleep.

Stepping into Shakespeare © Cambridge University Press 2000. See notice on p. ii

The Tempest Farewell to the audience

STORY

Prospero speaks this speech at the end of the masque to celebrate the engagement of his daughter, Miranda, and Prince Ferdinand. But you can use it as the final 'scene' or 'curtain call' for any school Shakespeare course. The speech gives pupils a very clear objective: to make a dramatic and memorable farewell to their audience.

CHARACTERS

PROSPERO Duke of Milan (but the pupils can speak as themselves to conclude any dramatic presentation)

LANGUAGE

revels play-acting, entertainments
baseless fabric unreal contents
insubstantial pageant
    unreal scene, little play
rack wisp of cloud

Prospero's 11 lines offer an excellent opportunity for choral speaking or individual performance. The vocabulary, rhythm and evocative imagery of the speech enable pupils to speak and perform a moving farewell to their audience.

TEACHING SUGGESTIONS

Whole class

Have three or four pupil volunteers stand behind you (or alongside you) as actors. Speak the speech a short section at a time, with all the class repeating your words and gestures. Some suggestions:

- 'Our revels now are ended' – you and the actors take a bow.
- 'These our actors' – a sweeping gesture to indicate the actors.
- 'As I foretold you' – point to your lips, then to the 'audience'.
- 'were all spirits' – actors freeze into dramatic poses (as 'king', 'soldier', etc.).
- 'and Are melted into air' – actors unfreeze and drop heads, eyes closed.
- 'into thin air' – another gesture, actors turn to face away from class.

Carry on in this way, using hand gestures and your actors' movements to indicate 'baseless fabric' (spread or sweep hands), 'cloud-capped towers' (point up), 'gorgeous palaces' (bowing and scraping), 'solemn temples' (hands in prayer). If your pupils have studied the Globe Theatre, and there is a picture of it in the room, point to that on 'the great globe itself'. Give 'shall dissolve' and 'this insubstantial pageant faded' a sad feeling of finality.

- 'We are such stuff As dreams are made on' – emphasise 'we', and indicate audience (to include everyone), then raise hand to head as if drowsy.
- 'and our little life Is rounded with a sleep' – everyone ends with eyes closed.

Group work

Groups of any size prepare their presentation of the lines. If they have been working on a particular play, they can present themselves as the characters in that play, freezing into characteristic postures.

Independent work

Use any worksheet from pages 96–107.

OR

Learn the speech by heart and speak it in a class festival.

As You Like It
The seven ages of man

All the world's a stage,
And all the men and women merely players.
They have their exits and their entrances,
And one man in his time plays many parts,
His acts being seven ages. At first the infant,
Mewling and puking in the nurse's arms.
Then the whining schoolboy with his satchel
And shining morning face, creeping like snail
Unwillingly to school. And then the lover,
Sighing like a furnace, with a woeful ballad
Made to his mistress' eyebrow. Then a soldier,
Full of strange oaths, and bearded like the pard,
Jealous in honour, sudden, and quick in quarrel,
Seeking the bubble reputation
Even in the cannon's mouth. And then the justice,
In fair round belly with good capon lined,
With eyes severe, and beard of formal cut,
Full of wise saws and modern instances,
And so he plays his part. The sixth age shifts
Into the lean and slippered pantaloon,
With spectacles on nose and pouch on side,
His youthful hose, well-saved, a world too wide
For his shrunk shank, and his big, manly voice
Turning again to childish treble, pipes
And whistles in his sound. Last scene of all
That ends this strange, eventful history,
Is second childishness and mere oblivion,
Sans teeth, sans eyes, sans taste, sans everything.

As You Like It The seven ages of man

STORY

In *As You Like It*, Jaques tells of the seven ages of man from infancy to extreme old age.

CHARACTERS

INFANT and NURSE
SCHOOLBOY
LOVER
SOLDIER
JUSTICE a judge
PANTALOON a feeble old man
VERY OLD MAN

LANGUAGE

players actors
Mewling and puking
    crying and being sick
woeful ballad
    sad poem or song
pard leopard
Jealous in honour
    fiercely concerned for respect
sudden violent
bubble reputation
    short-lasting fame
capon chicken
wise saws proverbs
modern instances
    everyday sayings
pantaloon feeble old man
hose stockings
shrunk shank withered leg
sans without

The brief but imagination-stirring descriptions are inviting opportunities for pupils to act out each of the seven ages. The speech is an extended image of human life as being like actors on a stage. There are striking similes ('like snail', 'like a furnace', etc.) and metaphors ('exits and entrances', 'shining morning face', 'bubble reputation', etc.).

TEACHING SUGGESTIONS

Whole class

The speech divides up into its introduction (first four and a half lines) and each of the seven ages. Speak a short section at a time with all pupils repeating your language actions. Some teaching suggestions are given on pages 4–5; here are others which can help your delivery:

- introduction – at least eight actions ('stage', 'men', 'women', 'players', 'exits', 'entrances', 'many parts', 'seven ages').

- infant – act as the nurse, rocking the baby in your arms, and reacting to the baby vomiting over you ('puking').

- schoolboy – show 'satchel', 'shining morning face', 'creeping like snail'. Ask the pupils to show how they come to school!

- lover – sigh; 'write' an imaginary poem; look besotted.

- soldier – make the oaths really strange (but not obscene!); stroke your beard; look haughty, violent and brave (pose as if you are charging the enemy).

- justice – rub stomach, accept bribe (judges sometimes had their pockets 'lined' with the bribe of a chicken); look severe and speak some proverbs (e.g. 'a stitch in time saves nine') and everyday sayings (e.g. 'have a nice day').

- pantaloon – stoop, peer short-sightedly, speak in a high treble voice.

- extreme old age – follow Shakespeare's description!

For younger pupils it is important that they enjoy the speech and act out the seven ages. You may also find an appropriate time for pupils to question the truth of Shakespeare's portrayal of human life. Is it very pessimistic and cynical? Choose your discussion time carefully. Don't be over-serious.

Group work

The task for each group is to prepare a presentation of the speech. Groups can be of almost any size, because pupils can 'double' the parts they act out. It is usually best for each group to have a narrator (or narrators) to speak the lines (with many pauses) as other pupils act out the descriptions of the seven ages.

Independent work

Use any worksheet from pages 96–107.

OR

Either write 'The seven ages of woman', or 'The seven ages of a school pupil'.

Romeo and Juliet
Queen Mab

She is the fairies' midwife, and she comes
In shape no bigger than an agate-stone
On the forefinger of an alderman,
Drawn with a team of little atomies,
Athwart men's noses as they lie asleep.
Her wagon spokes made of long spinners' legs,
The cover, of the wings of grasshoppers.
Her traces, of the moonshine's watery beams,
Her collar of the smallest spider web.
Her whip of cricket bone, the lash of film.
Her waggoner, a small gray-coated gnat.
Her chariot is an empty hazelnut
Made by the joiner squirrel or old grub
Time out of mind the fairies' coach-maker.
And in this state she gallops night by night
Through lovers' brains and then they dream on love;
O'er courtiers knees, that dream on curtsies straight.
O'er ladies' lips, who straight on kisses dream
Which oft the angry Mab with blisters plagues
Because their breaths with sweetmeats tainted are.
Sometime she gallops o'er a lawyer's lip
And then dreams he of smelling out a suit.
And sometimes comes she with a tithe-pig's tail,
Tickling a parson's nose as he lies asleep,
Then dreams he of another benefice.
Sometime she driveth o'er a soldier's neck,
And then dreams he of cutting foreign throats,
Of breaches, ambuscados, Spanish blades,
Of healths five fathom deep; and then anon
Drums in his ear, at which he starts and wakes,
And being thus frighted, swears a prayer or two,
And sleeps again.

Romeo and Juliet Queen Mab

STORY

In *Romeo and Juliet*, **Mercutio gives a vivid description of Queen Mab. He tells how she visits sleepers, giving them fantastic dreams.**

CHARACTERS

QUEEN MAB maker of dreams
LOVERS, COURTIERS, LADIES,
LAWYERS, PARSONS, SOLDIERS

LANGUAGE

agate-stone jewel in ring
alderman local politician
atomies specks of dust
Athwart across
spinners spiders
traces reins
straight immediately
suit legal case
tithe-pig pig given to the church
benefice profitable parish
breaches holes in defences
ambuscados ambushes
Spanish blades swords
healths drinking toasts (cheers!)

The speech comprises two long lists: the fantastically detailed description of Queen Mab's tiny chariot, and the dreams she causes in different sleepers. Both lists offer imaginatively creative opportunities for pupils.

TEACHING SUGGESTIONS

Whole class

It can be helpful to begin with a discussion of dreams. What are they like? What causes them? Then tell the pupils they are going to meet Queen Mab, the maker of dreams. Speak the speech in short sections with pupils repeating your words and any actions. The following can help your delivery:

- The first 14 lines are a very detailed description of Queen Mab and her coach. The lines can be inspiration for design activity (see Independent work below). Use a tone of voice (precise, intense) and add gestures to emphasise the tiny and delicate nature of Mab and her chariot.

- Not all the items mentioned in the speech appear in the picture on the pupils' script. As you speak, ask pupils to identify items on their own copies of the script, but help them with those which are missing ('team', 'spokes', 'cover').

- The last 18 lines describe different dreamers, and the dreams that Queen Mab causes them to have. Add appropriate actions as you speak. The pupils can model your actions or invent their own as they repeat each short section after you:

lovers	dream of	love
courtiers	dream of	'curtsies' (bowing and scraping)
ladies	dream of	kisses
a lawyer	dreams of	a profitable legal case
a parson	dreams of	another parish that will enrich him
a soldier	dreams of	military action and hard drinking

Group work

Groups of five or more prepare a presentation of the speech which shows Queen Mab visiting each of the dreamers. The first 14 lines can be chorally spoken, with or without actions. The final 18 lines should be accompanied with actions to illustrate what each dreamer is seeing and experiencing in their dream.

Independent work

Use any worksheet from pages 96–107.

OR

Use the first 14 lines to design your image of Queen Mab and her coach.

OR

Write ten lines of verse describing your own dreams.

The Two Gentlemen of Verona
A hard-hearted dog

I think Crab, my dog, be the sourest-natured dog that lives. My mother weeping, my father wailing, my sister crying, our maid howling, our cat wringing her hands, and all our house in great perplexity, yet did not this cruel-hearted cur shed one tear.

He is a stone, a very pebble-stone, and has he no more pity in him than a dog. Why, my grandam, having no eyes, look you, wept herself blind at my parting. Nay, I'll show you the manner of it.

This shoe is my father. No, this left shoe is my father. No, no, this left shoe is my mother. Nay, that cannot be so, neither. Yes it is so, it is so, it hath the worser sole. This shoe with the hole in it is my mother, and this my father. A vengeance on't, there 'tis. Now sir, this staff is my sister, for, look you, she is as white as a lily and as small as a wand. This hat is Nan, our maid. I am the dog. No, the dog is himself and I am the dog. O, the dog is me and I am myself. Ay, so, so.

Now come I to my father, 'Father your blessing'. Now should not the shoe speak a word for weeping. Now should I kiss my father. Well, he weeps on. Now come I to my mother. O that she could speak now like a wood woman. Well, I kiss her. Well, there 'tis. Here's my mother's breath up and down. Now come I to my sister. Mark the moan she makes. – Now the dog all this while sheds not a tear nor speaks a word. But see how I lay the dust with my tears.

Stepping into Shakespeare © Cambridge University Press 2000. See notice on p. ii

STORY

In *The Two Gentlemen of Verona*, Lance, about to go on a journey, describes how he said farewell to his family and his dog, Crab. Everyone weeps except Crab.

CHARACTERS

LANCE a servant
CRAB his dog
Pupils may choose to have Lance's mother, father, sister, grandmother, maid and cat in the action!

LANGUAGE

perplexity disturbance
grandam grandmother
sole sole of shoe (or soul)
A vengeance on't
    the devil take it!
staff walking-stick
wand white stick
wood woman mad, furious

Lance is like a stand-up comedian, telling a long story to make the audience laugh. Shakespeare gives him prose (because in his plays servants usually did not speak verse) and puts all kinds of repetitions, contradictions and absurdities into the story to increase the fun.

TEACHING SUGGESTIONS

Whole class

This is definitely not a Shakespeare speech to take too seriously. Lance describes how his family – and his dog – behaved at his departure from Verona. Shakespeare intends Lance to amuse the audience, so step into role and speak his speech straight through to give pupils a first impression.

You will need a pair of shoes, a staff (a stick or ruler) a hat and a 'dog' played by a pupil (or use a stuffed toy, or drawing of a dog).

As you speak the first paragraph, identify individual pupils in the class as mother, father, sister, maid – and cat! Those pupils perform the actions described ('my mother weeping, my father wailing, my sister crying, our maid howling, our cat wringing her hands'). Make sure that the pupil playing the 'dog' stays impassive throughout ('He is a stone, a very pebble-stone …').

For the last two paragraphs of the speech, address all your remarks to the shoes (father and mother), staff (sister) or hat (maid), but you might choose to hand the articles to the pupils playing those parts. Use the shoes to show how Lance gets muddled up as he tries to match them with his father and mother. Emphasise the very bad pun on 'sole' (soul). Bring out Lance's confusion as he mixes up himself up with the dog.

Let the punctuation be your guide. Speak in short sections, and leave yourself and the pupils plenty of time to demonstrate each action. A key to the humour in this speech is to make sure that each short phrase counts, so use plenty of pauses for action and reaction.

Group work

Because this is a comic scene it is best not to over-explain, but to give pupils the opportunity to speak the lines themselves so that they can directly experience how the language creates the laughter.

Pupils work in threes and take turn to speak as Lance. As he tells his story one pupil acts as Crab the dog, and the other acts out as many descriptions as possible. Alternatively, pupils can work in larger groups and share out the 'family' roles.

Independent work

Use any worksheet from pages 96–107.

OR

Write Crab's account of how he watched his master saying farewell to his family.

The Sonnets
Sonnet 18

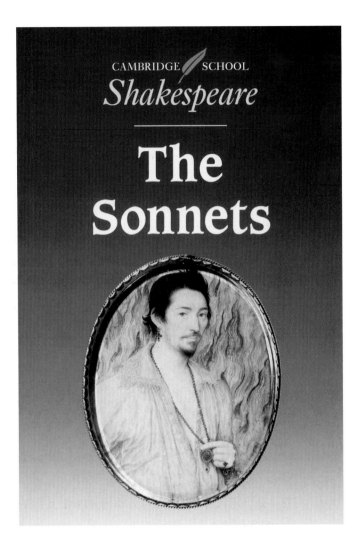

Shall I compare thee to a summer's day?
Thou art more lovely and more temperate.
Rough winds do shake the darling buds of May,
And summer's date hath all too short a lease.
Sometime too hot the eye of heaven shines,
And often is his gold complexion dimmed;
And every fair from fair sometime declines,
By chance or nature's changing course untrimmed.
But thy eternal summer shall not fade,
Nor lose possession of that fair thou ow'st,
Nor shall Death brag thou wand'rst in his shade,
When in eternal lines to time thou grow'st.
So long as men can breathe or eyes can see,
So long lives this, and this gives life to thee.

Stepping into Shakespeare © Cambridge University Press 2000. See notice on p. ii

STORY

Sonnet 18 claims that the person who Shakespeare loves is more beautiful than a summer's day. Summer is short-lived, subject to rough weather and change. But the beauty of Shakespeare's beloved will triumph over death itself, living forever in this sonnet.

CHARACTERS

The 'characters' are the speaker of the sonnet and the person he or she loves.

LANGUAGE

temperate calm, even-tempered
lease duration
eye of heaven sun
nature's changing course
   the changing seasons
untrimmed robbed of beauty
   (stripped of ornament)
fair beauty
ow'st own
brag boast
eternal lines
   this immortal sonnet
to time thou grow'st
   you and time become one
   (are both eternal)

Sonnet 18 is written in perfectly regular iambic pentameter, and so provides the opportunity to teach Shakespeare's verse rhythm.

TEACHING SUGGESTIONS

Whole class

Because a sonnet is a poem, not a play, there are fewer opportunities to act out the lines. So treat Sonnet 18 as a poem and speak it line by line with the class repeating each line after you. To help pupils with the rhythm, emphasise the regular five-beat pattern in each line (the emphasis is marked by /):

/   /   /   /   /
Shall I compare thee to a summer's day?

The pupils can clap or tap out the rhythm as they speak, or move their hands or bodies gently, swaying with the rhythm. Every line has this regular five-beat pattern. You may wish to tell your pupils that this is called 'iambic pentameter'. Some pupils enjoy a longer explanation, and you can find it on page 7.

Shakespeare's sonnets have a very clear structure. Each sonnet has 14 lines, arranged as:

* three stanzas, each of four lines
* a final couplet of two lines.

Each stanza contains a 'thought' or idea. In Sonnet 18 these are:

* Stanza 1 (lines 1–4) – you are more beautiful than a summer's day. Summer lasts only a short time.
* Stanza 2 (lines 5–8) – the sun is sometimes too hot or clouded over, and all beauty fades.
* Stanza 3 (lines 9–12) – but your beauty will never fade or die. This sonnet will make you immortal.
* Couplet (lines 13–14) – as long as anyone is alive, they will see your beauty in this sonnet.

To help pupils discuss the meaning of the sonnet, take one line at a time and ask what picture it calls up in their minds. The sonnet is full of vivid images: 'darling buds of May' (why 'darling'?), 'the eye of heaven' (the sun), etc. which pupils can use as springboards for their own creativity.

Group work

In pairs or small groups, pupils take turns to read the sonnet to each other, emphasising the rhythm. They invent different opening lines in the same style ('Shall I compare thee to a ...?').

Independent work

Sonnet 18 provides wonderful encouragement for pupils to write their own poems, because it claims that poetry and what it describes can live for ever. So invite pupils to write their own sonnets using Sonnet 18 as their model.

Storyboard your scene

NAME	DATE
PLAY	
SCENE	

Imagine you are going to film your scene. Film-makers prepare a storyboard: a series of pictures showing each moment the camera will film, together with the language from the script. Choose six moments from your script and draw the picture in each box. Write the language the camera will capture on the dotted lines.

1

....
....

2

....
....

3

....
....

4

....
....

5

....
....

6

....
....

Stepping into Shakespeare © Cambridge University Press 2000. See notice on p. ii

What's your title?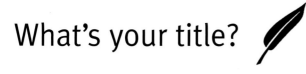

NAME		DATE
PLAY		
SCENE		

Storytellers and poets often use Shakespeare as the inspiration for their stories and poems. Their imagination is set working by a single line or phrase (a few words), and it becomes the title of their story or poem. What is your favourite line or phrase in this scene? Use it as the title of your own poem or story.

Title

....

Step into character!

NAME		DATE
PLAY		
SCENE		

Choose a character from your scene and step into role!

This is a drawing of what

.... ,

my character, is wearing:

This is the line I most enjoy speaking:

....

....

....

because

....

....

....

This is how I play my part and speak my lines. I begin by

....

....

....

....

Then I

....

....

....

....

Finally, I

....

....

....

....

These are the secret thoughts of my character:

....

....

....

Stepping into Shakespeare © Cambridge University Press 2000. See notice on p. ii

Become an actor at the Globe!

NAME		DATE
PLAY		
SCENE		

Turn the clock back to Shakespeare's time! You are an actor in Shakespeare's own acting company, the King's Men. Imagine you have played in the scene at the Globe. Write the letter you send to a friend shortly after the performance. Your letter includes:

- how you joined Shakespeare's company
- how you were selected for the part you played
- advice Mr Shakespeare gave you to help you act the part
- how you played the part (e.g. which lines you thought you spoke particularly well, your movements and gestures, any mistakes, etc.)
- your costume and any props
- how the audience responded.

Start your letter here and continue on other sheets.

Director's notes

NAME	DATE
PLAY	
SCENE	

Imagine you are the director of the scene. A director gives advice to the actors to help their performances.
Write your notes in the boxes below.

Names of the characters in the scene:

My advice to each character (e.g. how they enter, speak, move and so on):

This is what happens in the scene:

How the scene will end (the final stage picture that I want the audience to see):

The mood I want to create in this scene:

Stepping into Shakespeare © Cambridge University Press 2000. See notice on p. ii

Become a designer

NAME		DATE	
PLAY			
SCENE			

Select a character and design their costume. Describe your design and say why you chose it for your character.

Name of character:

....

Draw your costume design here:

Description of costume:

....
....
....
....
....
....
....
....
....
....
....
....

I have designed

....'s

costume like this because:

....
....
....
....
....
....
....
....
....
....
....

Invent a narrator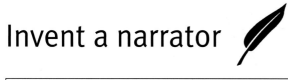

NAME	DATE
PLAY	
SCENE	

The role of the narrator is to speak directly to the audience. The narrator speaks at the beginning and end of the scene, and adds comments at different moments of the action. Write your script for the narrator to speak, telling the story, introducing the characters and helping the audience.

Here's how my narrator introduces the scene:

....

....

....

....

....

....

What my narrator says at different moments in the scene:

....

....

....

....

....

....

....

Here is what my narrator says at the end of the scene, to summarise what has happened, and to ask the audience to think about what may happen next:

....

....

....

....

....

....

....

Stepping into Shakespeare © Cambridge University Press 2000. See notice on p. ii

You are William Shakespeare!

NAME	DATE
PLAY	
SCENE	

Imagine you are William Shakespeare. Write your diary entry for what happened on one day when you rehearsed your scene in the morning, and played before an audience in the afternoon.

Today, I rehearsed the actors for (name of scene)

....

Here is the advice I gave them:

Write your review

NAME	DATE
PLAY	
SCENE	

Step back in time and imagine you have just seen your scene acted on the stage of Shakespeare's Globe Theatre. Write your review of what you saw. Describe:

- how the Globe audience behaved before the performance began

- what the performance was like (how the actors spoke their lines, how they entered, their costumes, etc.)

- which moments you particularly enjoyed or did not enjoy, and the reasons why you liked or disliked them

- your judgement of the entire performance.

Edit your newspaper

NAME	DATE
PLAY	
SCENE	

Create the front page of your own newspaper that reports the events of your scene. Use some of Shakespeare's language in your reporting. Your front page should include:

- name of your newspaper
- main headline and story
- picture to illustrate main story with a caption
- two short news items, each with a headline
- an advertisement.

Design a handbill

NAME	DATE
PLAY	
SCENE	

Shakespeare did not have television or newspapers to advertise his plays at the Globe. His Acting Company probably used handbills to give details of the forthcoming performances. Design a handbill to advertise your production. It should be eye-catching. Make people really want to come to see the play! Your handbill should include the following features:

- title of play
- where and when? (theatre, day and time)
- actors, and the characters they will play
- an exciting summary of what the audience will see
- special features of your production (costumes, effects, etc.)
- price of admission.

How I judge my work

NAME	DATE
PLAY	
SCENE	

What I did in the lesson
(e.g. the character I played):

....

I most enjoyed:

....

....

....

because

....

....

....

I least enjoyed:

....

....

....

because

....

....

....

Here are some of the things I learned in
the lesson:

....

....

....

....

....

....

....

This is how I judge my work rate in the
lesson (put a tick in one box):

☐ *I worked hard all through the lesson.*
☐ *I worked hard for most of the lesson.*
☐ *I worked hard for some of the lesson.*
☐ *I only worked a few times.*
☐ *I didn't work hard at all.*

This is how I helped other pupils:

....

....

....

....

This is how I judge my achievement:

....

....

....

....

....

This is what I need to do in the next
lesson to help my learning:

....

....

....

....

....

....

Successful school Shakespeare

PRINCIPLES

Successful Shakespeare teaching with younger pupils involves a combination of whole class, group and individual activities. It is based on the following principles:

- The teacher has high expectations and regard for pupils' contributions, performance, progress and achievement.

- All pupils take part in practical activities and discussion.

- Teachers and pupils recognise that Shakespeare's language is dramatic language to be acted out in some way. They treat it as a script to be spoken, explored physically and creatively, and brought to active life in some kind of performance.

- Pupils are encouraged and enabled to draw upon their own experience and culture to contribute to each lesson. This learner-centred approach develops pupils' sense of ownership of Shakespeare's language, characters and stories.

- Teachers have clear objectives which promote pupils' understanding and skills.

- Teachers use imaginative and collaborative strategies in a well-paced progression of varied activities throughout each lesson.

- Pupils are 'on task' throughout each lesson, having Shakespeare's stories, language and characters as the major focus of their activities.

A NOTE ON OBJECTIVES

This handbook has a common aim for every lesson: that pupils enjoy and understand Shakespeare's stories, characters and language. It also recognises that every lesson should have clear objectives. Such objectives include enabling pupils to master metaphor or simile, alliteration or assonance, verse rhythm, rhyme, word order, use of suffixes or prefixes or hyphens, and many other language techniques. But Shakespeare presents a special problem in setting objectives because every script contains a wealth of possibilities. For example each script in this collection contains vivid imagery which can be used to fire pupils' imagination, to understand how metaphor, simile or personification works, and to develop their own literacy skills. In addition, every script has other distinctive language features that might provide an objective for the lesson.

The teacher's notes provided with each script identify the particular language characteristics of that script. They specify for example where a script is particularly valuable in teaching a specific skill or technique (e.g. pages 24 and 94 for the verse rhythm of iambic pentameter, or page 28 for alliteration). The notes are offered in the knowledge that each teacher will use his or her professional judgement to decide which particular objectives are appropriate to their own pupils at any moment in their Shakespeare course. Teachers can use the notes to select their objective or objectives for each lesson. Long experience confirms that teachers are wisely wary of over-analysis of Shakespeare's language, and use their judgement to ensure that over-concentration on a particular objective does not destroy pupils' enjoyment.

MORE IDEAS?

Are you looking for additional practical ideas for use with younger pupils in your classroom? You will find a host of suggestions in every Cambridge School Shakespeare edition of each play which you can adapt to the needs, abilities and interests of your pupils.